Creativity
and the Autistic Student

Creativity

and the Autistic Student

Supporting Strengths to Develop Skills and Deepen Knowledge

Carrie C. Snow

TEACHERS COLLEGE PRESS

TEACHERS COLLEGE | COLUMBIA UNIVERSITY

NEW YORK AND LONDON

Published by Teachers College Press, 1234 Amsterdam Avenue, New York, NY 10027

Library of Congress Cataloging-in-Publication Data is available at loc.gov

ISBN 978-0-8077-5727-7 (paper)
ISBN 978-0-8077-5728-4 (hardcover)
ISBN 978-0-8077-7425-0 (ebook)

Printed on acid-free paper
Manufactured in the United States of America

22 21 20 19 18 17 16 15   8 7 6 5 4 3 2 1

For Dave, Sabine, Mario

Contents

Acknowledgments

The writing of this book has been a process of attempting to contribute meaningful work to a field I love, and that has nourished my life for many years. Many people have helped make this work possible. I extend gratitude to the editorial team at Teachers College Press: Emily Renwick, Jennifer Baker, Noelle De-La-Paz, and especially Brian Ellerbeck, whose early response of interest in my book idea was incredibly encouraging. In sustaining a belief in the work, Brian played an important role in my transformation from a fledgling book writer to a published author. Meg Hartmann patiently helped me navigate the learning curve of submitting a book proposal to the Press. The anonymous peer reviewers offered generous insights that nudged me to explore different approaches to writing the book. Susan Liddicoat provided thorough, straightforward, and comprehensive editing that improved my presentation in a way that honored my ideas and voice. For these skills and for her accessibility and flexibility throughout the editing process, I am grateful.

The early renderings of my proposal were benefitted by the astute eyes of Susan Baglieri, Jacqueline Leber, and Rachel Oppenheim, three friends, scholars, and former colleagues whom I respect immensely. I thank them for the time they took from their busy lives to read and respond to my early work.

The book is enlivened and enriched by the insights of the very generous, spirited, and articulate people with whom I shared email dialogues. I am indebted to Henry Goldsmith, Vincent Mazzone, Sarah Gaines, and Tito Mukhopadhyay for sharing their thoughts, ideas, and work with me for purposes of improving life in school for autistic youth. Similarly, I am grateful for the many sources I referenced in this book, including scholars and autistic artists and writers. The immense contributions that each has given to their field benefit many. I count myself among those who are lucky enough to have learned from the creativity of the autistic artists and writers who are represented in this book.

My husband Dave has shown leagues of patience and flexibility through this process. Tackling this project while in the midst of raising two young kids proved that creative work definitely does rely on collaborative efforts. I extend heartfelt gratitude to Dave, who is the best partner I can imagine. Finally, I thank my daughter Sabine and son Mario, for the joy, vitality, and endless curve balls they bring to our lives; and my mom, sister, and parents-in-law, who have given me support and encouragement in spades.

Preface

I have written *Creativity and the Autistic Student* for those preparing to become teachers, those who currently teach, and those who administrate
in elementary and secondary schools. This book bears relevance for educators who are specialists (e.g., special education, art), as well as those
who are generalists. My focus is on certain key qualities of education that
commonly are cited by autistic people as significant to their development
of fulfilling lives, healthy identities, promising careers and vocations, and
creativity in general. These key qualities can be applied flexibly to support the creative development of autistic students in K–12 classrooms and
schools, whether they are public or private, inclusive or specialized. Yet
this book is grounded on the principles of inclusion, for I believe that the
potential for the most democratic and equitable educational experiences
is encountered in classrooms that represent an array of abilities, experiences, and ways of being. I recognize that inclusion is not an easy route,
and is one that relies on the coordination and cooperation of teachers,
families, administrators, and students.

DEVELOPMENT OF MY UNDERSTANDINGS
ABOUT AUTISM AND EDUCATION

Spanning more than 15 years, my work in the field of special education has included tutoring, mentoring, classroom teaching, educational
research, student teaching supervision, and teacher education. My perspective likewise is tempered by parenting two young children who are
growing up in a different age than that in which I first began my career. In the 1990s, students deemed in need of special education typically
were taught in self-contained classrooms or specialized schools, yet mainstreaming was becoming a model that some schools used. Often, mainstreaming meant that students deemed in need of special education spent
part of their day in a general education classroom, but most of the day
in their self-contained classroom. Often it meant that they spent no time
in general education classrooms, but joined general education peers for
lunch and recess. This model was inching toward what is now referred to

as inclusion, where the idea is that students with individualized education plans are integrated with their general education peers, sharing classes on a full-time basis. While clear strides have been made, there is still a lot of work to be done in efforts to create inclusive, equitable learning experiences for all youth. Yet I remain optimistic that we will continue to build on the progress we have made thus far. I need only to contrast my own childhood school experiences with those of my children to realize that although there is much yet to do, inclusive practices have given youth of varying abilities the chance to get to know one another. As a child growing up in the 1980s, if there were autistic students in my school, I did not know it. While common practice then was to segregate students deemed in need of special education from their general education peers (to be taught in portable classrooms outside of the main building), the reality was that there was little interfacing between "us" and "them." This structure of segregation offered no possibility for either group to get to know the other in any genuine way.

As my oldest child navigates public school as a kindergartner, I witness what she learns about what autism means in the context of her inclusive classroom. Her impression that an autistic classmate, who is a very strong math student, "knows more than the rest of us," shores up my optimism that the quality of life in school for autistic youth is beginning to change for the better. Just as important is the reality that the quality of life in school for neurotypical students (such as my daughter) likewise is changing for the better. With integration, neurotypical students benefit from getting to know autistic youth and learning from the strengths and qualities they contribute to the classroom community. Each of my roles has contributed to my understanding of the systems that support and hinder the success of autistic students in schools. Throughout my immersion in the field of special education, I have always been especially drawn to the perspectives of students. They offer fresh ideas that bring currency, relevance, and heart to issues that are typically dominated by educational professionals. Whether they realize it or not, students are unique experts who can give richly, namely by providing insights into facets of their educational experiences that worked or failed to work for them. I found this to be the case during a previous study that directly influenced my interest in undertaking this current project.

In the fall of 2007, I began data collection in two high schools (one public, one private) in a large U.S. city. I set out to work with three students with Asperger syndrome (AS) in an effort to understand from their perspectives what schooling meant to them. Over the course of 6 months, I observed the students in various classroom contexts, walked with them between classes, and traversed the city searching for dry, warm places to sit and talk about their school-based lives. I found that their experiences were often in contrast to common stories conveyed about AS. Of particular interest to me was the finding that the students engaged in a number of creative strategies in their efforts to make sense of their social and academic worlds.

However, my interest in the relationship between autism and creativity can be traced back even further and perhaps has its earliest roots in my experience as a classroom teacher. Five years prior to the 2007 study, and in the same city, I was a teacher working with upper elementary autistic students. These youth revealed, in their actions, words, goals, and dreams, the many ways in which they defied the stereotypes I had come to know as hallmarks of their classification. While they were supposed to represent flat or "stiff" emotionality (Myles & Simpson, 2001, p. 2), these students were perhaps the most emotionally expressive people I had ever met in my life. This emotionality was evident, for instance, in the way one boy inflected his voice when reading to the class, emulating each character with varying pitch and tonality. It was likewise evident in the depth of laughter that many of the students expressed when something was funny. One student ran away or hid under a desk when he felt fearful, anxious, or otherwise overwhelmed. Another often stormed in anger to retreat behind the curtain of the "quiet space" we had set up in the classroom for times when students needed a break. Their feelings were very much out in the open, and anything but stiff.

Furthermore, although the social impairment of my autistic students had been delineated (American Psychiatric Association, 2000), I noticed their sense of loyalty to one another, as if they were siblings. Like siblings, there were tensions and plenty of instances of arguing and fighting, sometimes even to violent ends. But despite these growing pains, the students were close. Permanently etched in my memory is a vision of my class huddled together on the evening of their elementary school graduation. In that quiet moment, they communicated a strong sense of connectedness and seemed to pay honor to the years they had grown up together, shaped one another, supported one another. And now, with collective apprehension and excitement, they were letting go of one another. About to disperse to different middle schools throughout the city, they held tight one last time to the familiarity they had grown to count on.

While I always noticed attributes in my students that strayed quite far from those outlined in professional diagnostic manuals and popular media alike, the sense of imagination and creativity that the students demonstrated on a daily basis resonated with me deeply. Although not always the case, many of their interests were centered on artistic, creative endeavors such as playing an instrument or drawing. Some expressed creativity by attending to personal style such as putting together outfits that set them apart in a unique way from their peers. As is true for all students, I noticed that when my students referenced their creative interests, new learning became relevant and meaningful. It was a process of making new use of "old" material, of constructing novelty from a wellspring of tried-and-true knowledge. This forging of the old with the new was a process in which each student engaged, and it struck me that in this way each demonstrated creative capacity on a daily basis. The fact that these students were regularly engaging in creativity is not surprising except that the overwhelming message (in scholarship and popular media) about autistic people is that, above all, their supposed rigidity and preference for familiarity reigns over any interest they may have in novelty.

OBSERVATIONS FROM SUSTAINED RELATIONSHIPS

Today, I remain in contact with some of my former students and research participants who are now adults pursuing college degrees and looking for jobs. Some have contributed to this book, in the form of new data that I share in Chapter 3. The sustained nature of the relationships I have with these individuals has been gratifying and has allowed me to bear witness to their negotiation of numerous influences and, through these negotiations, to their construction of identities and fulfilling lives for themselves. As they have entered early adulthood, it has been revealing to see how many of these individuals have carved paths that revolve around their creative endeavors, including illustration, theater performance, and music. This reality suggests the very crucial role that creative expression has played in their successful navigation through childhood and adolescence to reach young adulthood with a positive sense of self in place.

My interest in the relationship between autism and creativity has led me beyond my former students to the work of other, more well-known autistic people, many of whom I reference and feature in this book. These individuals evidence new ways of perceiving and interpreting the world, often through creative processes such as poetry and painting. Sometimes these perceptions and interpretations are revealed through gestures or speech. Through a variety of creative expression, these people have contributed to a strengths-based understanding of autism.

LANGUAGE USAGE OF PERSONAL DESCRIPTORS

The strengths-based interpretation that so many autistic people (and their allies) have cultivated is reflected in a recent linguistic shift. Many people who are active in autism self-advocacy communities have led the way in shifting the language from person-first to identity-first (i.e., from "person with autism" to "autistic person") as an act of self-acceptance. In light of this development, I have come to understand autism as a lens through which one experiences life in a way similar to temperament. For example, a primary disposition of extroversion filters one's life experiences and perceptions holistically, as does one of primary introversion (see Cain, 2012). The people who are featured in this book attest to this reality. They show how the neurological wiring that manifests broadly as "autism" offers both new angles and distinct tensions through which to understand human experience in its diversity. In this book, I align with autism advocacy communities and adopt the usage of identity-first language, referring to those featured in this book as "autistic people." I make this decision in regard to autism distinctly, since autism advocacy groups have made such a concerted appeal for adopting identity-first language. When referring to disability in general, however, I continue to use person-first language.

I realize that the change in vernacular to identity-first brings discomfort for many people who remain tied to person-first language. This is understandable: Person-first language came in response to oppressive language that defined people in terms of their supposed inabilities. The move to person-first language was undoubtedly a critical step in shifting the focus from the disability to the person. However, person-first language can have the effect of distancing the disability from the person, where the disability can feel like an add-on feature to a person's life as opposed to an integral and important part of the person's identity. With regard to autism, I make the shift from person-first to identity-first language as a way to support the strides that many autistic people have made in deciding how they are represented in the world. I also make the choice in acknowledgment that for many individuals autism is a source of pride.

OVERVIEW OF THIS BOOK

The chapters that follow highlight some of the many contributions autistic people have made to a young yet evolving understanding of autism and creativity. There are a few instances (in Chapter 4) where I likewise reference my own experience as a classroom teacher of autistic elementary students, yet overwhelmingly the book is guided by the ideas set forth by the various autistic people herein represented. These contributions are given for the particular purpose of enhancing the quality of life in school for autistic youth. In the process of reinterpreting the relationship between autism and creativity, I weave creativity scholarship throughout the book and highlight its relevance for educational application.

In Chapter 1, I address the reason for undertaking a project of revising interpretations of autism and creativity for educational contexts. I lay out the foundations for the book, including a discussion of strengths-based conceptions of autism, the use of a Disability Studies stance, and an alignment with a neurodiversity perspective. Chapter 1 also contains a brief overview of how autistic students fit into the new diversity of contemporary inclusive classrooms, provides a discussion about common meanings of autism, and puts forth the conception that creativity is a quality common to all people.

Chapter 2 aligns autism with creativity through an exploration and analysis of creative ability in autistic people as gleaned through autism scholarship and autism autobiography. The chapter begins with a discussion and critique of the common framing of autism as indicative of exceptionality, a position that contrasts the common, deficit perspective outlined in Chapter 1. The discussion points to the need for narratives and interpretations that align autistic people as capable of the sort of everyday creativity that all people engage in on a regular basis. The exemplars shared in Chapter 2 shed light on a variety of everyday forms of creativity demonstrated by autistic people. Analysis of the body of autobiographical work is focused around several issues that the authors identify as significant to the educational lives of autistic people.

In Chapter 3, I turn to artistic forms of creativity as demonstrated by several autistic individuals. Here, the focal points are the skills, abilities, and qualities cultivated by engagement in arts-based creative work. These focal points structure the discussion of the artistic work represented in the chapter, and artists' insights illuminate how creative work enriches the quality of their lives in multiple ways.

Chapter 4 builds on the insights and ideas presented in Chapters 2 and 3. This chapter, addressed to educators, suggests a variety of strategies and practices to provide educational experiences that can help autistic students join their peers in developing their creative potential.

Finally, in Chapter 5, I discuss teaching for creativity in the current era and visions for a future that invites and thrives on the creative contributions of neurodiverse citizens.

What I have witnessed through my sustained relationships with autistic people, and discovered through research, is significantly disconnected from the common belief that autistic individuals are marked by an inability to imagine and create. In this book, I attempt to make sense of this disconnection. My understanding of what autism means, then, continues to evolve in this project. While my former students represent a luminous spark in my life as an educator, their insights and actions continue to propel the tilling of new soil. Writing this book is a way to honor the students who were truly my first teachers with regard to autism.

CHAPTER 1

The Relevance of Revising Interpretations of Autism and Creativity in Education Contexts

Creativity is not simply a property of exceptional people but an exceptional property of all people.

— Ron Carter (2004)

This book looks exclusively to autistic people and their allies to locate qualities that support, strengthen, and enhance the education of autistic youth. Using creative expression as a focal point, I discuss common ideas that autistic people share as important to their sense of identity, well-being, and quality of life. Their insights can provide a basis for constructing curricular experiences that are equitable, inclusive, and attentive to the specific attributes and sensitivities of autistic students. An integration of relevant creativity scholarship enriches the discussions that unfold in the coming chapters.

In the chapters that follow, I focus on ways that creative endeavors can aid and catalyze a number of important skills in the lives of autistic youth. Relatedly, I discuss how features associated with autism can dovetail with habits necessary for creative development. Throughout the book, I also attend to ways that autistic expression contributes uniquely to understandings of creative processes.

The book is guided by the insight and work of a variety of autistic people ranging in age from youth to adulthood. Many of these autistic people speak directly about the ways in which aspects of their school experiences supported or curtailed their ability to feel included in rich curricular experiences in conjunction with their diverse peers. Others do not directly address schooling but nonetheless contribute expressions of creativity and imagination that inspire ideas about how schooling experiences might be enriched.

As significant as artistic forms of creativity are the instances of creative expression that illuminate autistic individuals' innovative problem solving and negotiating day-to-day issues that arise. These "everyday" forms of creativity, like artistic forms, can help strengthen an alignment between autism and creativity.

In a broad sense, my work aims to disrupt dominant beliefs about the relationship between autism and creativity. Such a revision can contribute to a growing discourse in scholarship that focuses on autism as a way of being that represents strengths. Yet the focus on creativity in this book also has a distinct purpose for school-based application. Through the lens of creativity, educators can glean the ways that autistic students experience the world and discern what these students deem to be important. From there, educators can plan curricular experiences that bear relevance and meaning for their students' backgrounds, present lives, propensities, and futures.

This chapter contains an overview of features and values that shape and guide the book. I begin with a discussion of how the inclusion movement has played a role in developing a diverse American student body and then locate autistic students as a part of this new diversity. I then share common conceptions of autism as reflected in the *Diagnostic and Statistical Manual of Mental Disorders* (DSM). Next, I discuss a strengths-based understanding of autism and how aligning with Disability Studies (DS) and neurodiversity can support this stance. I move on to discuss how attending to personal interests can enrich educational opportunities and support creative development and identity formation of autistic youth. Next, I contend that seeing creativity as a process in which all people engage allows for an alignment to be made between autism and creativity. Finally, I share how recognizing a strengths-based conception of autism underlies understanding autism as concomitant with creative ability. The chapters that follow rest upon these foundational features and offer a generative exploration and analysis of autism and creativity. As the culminating chapters particularly demonstrate, this exploration bears implications for work in classrooms and schools.

INCLUSION AND A NEW DIVERSITY

In the past decade, American educators have become increasingly focused on the inclusion of students with disabilities in general education classrooms. Although the interpretation and enactment of this concept vary, the imperative behind inclusionary practices is to educate all students, in accordance with the Individuals with Disabilities Education Act (IDEA), in the least restrictive environment (LRE). Schools committed to inclusion have made attempts to move away from traditional models of special education, in which students with disabilities are educated in separate, self-contained classrooms. In joining their general education peers in classrooms, students with individual education plans have contributed to a changing landscape within American schools.

Implications for Educators

The growing diversity of students who represent differences in physical/motor ability, as well as intellectual, behavioral, or cognitive ability, has presented educators with an enormous task. In response to the challenge to meet the vast and varying needs of students who constitute this new diversity, structural modifications such as increased personnel support have been instrumental. The employment of paraprofessionals who work one-on-one with students in their classrooms is one example of a structural modification that has supported the work of inclusive-classroom teachers. Another is the use of an array of participation structures to ensure that students with diverse learning styles have equitable access to curricular experiences. Yet another example is the adoption of a collaborative team teaching (CTT) model, where certified general education and special education teachers work in tandem.

Flexibility in curricular design, namely differentiation, has been an indispensable tool teachers have used in efforts to help their students reach their learning potentials. A scheme for thinking about teaching and learning in flexible terms, differentiation involves considerations for modified curricula that increase students' ability to reach common educational goals. Differentiation takes several forms, for example:

- Engaging students using a multiplicity of modalities
- Enfolding personal interests into curricular goals
- Allowing flexibility in time taken to complete projects
- Having an openness to approaching the same problem in different ways
- Offering students various means to demonstrate their learning of common concepts

Autistic Students as Part of the New Diversity

As inclusionary practices have gained momentum over the past several years, implications have begun to surface for different groups of students. Contributing to the changing landscape of schools across the nation, autistic students represent a group that is entering general education classrooms at increasing rates. While the inclusion of autistic students has seen progress, there is still much to learn and to do to improve inclusionary practices (Kluth, 2003). Thomas Insel (2012), director of the National

Institute of Mental Health, reports that according to the Developmental Disabilities Services registry of California, services for autistic youth have increased twelvefold in the past 20 years. The growing prevalence of people who receive services related to autism translates to more and more lives touched by autism in some way or another. In the past 2 decades, there has been a deluge of information about, as well as broad interest in, what it means to be autistic. Broderick and Ne'eman (2008) refer to autism as an international "popular cultural obsession" (p. 462). This observation reflects the reality that autism has captured the interest of communities beyond education, academia, medicine, and science, as evidenced in popular culture media such as films (e.g., *Temple Grandin* [M. Jackson, 2010] and *Adam* [Mayer, 2009]) and works of literary fiction (e.g., Haddon, 2003, and Lord, 2006) that represent autism. In the classroom, a range of characteristics associated with autism can challenge educators' abilities to help these students reach their learning potentials. It follows that differentiating instruction for autistic students is an important concern for contemporary teachers, as evidenced by the success of texts that shed light on strategies for successful integration of autistic students into general education classrooms (e.g., Kluth, 2003).

The proliferation of those receiving services related to autism in recent years is reflected in research. Much of the work within the field of education focuses on ways that educators can help remediate behaviors of autistic students. These students typically are represented as generally rigid and lacking in abilities such as taking the perspective of others and engaging in socially "appropriate" ways. Framed in terms of these supposed deficiencies, autistic students often are depicted as impaired in the ability to imagine and create. The emphasis on remediation edges out discussions about ways in which creative engagement and the abilities it exposes and catalyzes can be recognized and supported to enhance school-based learning opportunities for autistic students.

COMMON CONCEPTIONS ABOUT AUTISM

The idea that autism is a condition to be remediated and cured has roots fixed in the *Diagnostic and Statistical Manual of Mental Disorders*, historically a foundational resource for autism classifications. The manual echoes the observations of psychiatrist Leo Kanner (1943) and pediatrician Hans Asperger (1944/1991), who were the first to contribute scholarly descriptions of autism. Asperger focused heavily on autistic youth who were verbal (hence the name Asperger syndrome, a classification that denotes an agility with speech) and who showed qualities of language use that were awkward or original. Kanner's work integrated more discussion of qualities that indicated a lack of agility with or unusual uses of speech, including mutism and echolalia (the latter of which entails the use of speech in a repetitious form). Each described the difficulties experienced by the children with whom he worked, such as inflexible imaginary play, stereotyped patterns of movement, and a preference for familiarity. While the descriptions that each contributed aligned in the majority of respects, they differed in tone and focus. Asperger's descriptions revealed a degree of nuance and a sense of thoughtful regard for the youth. For example, Asperger suggested that despite appearances that might suggest a disregard for others (such as eye contact that lasted for a brief moment), the autistic youth showed a keen awareness of their environment and, as constant observers of themselves, were actually quite self-conscious. In contrast, Kanner seems to have focused heavily on the children's social struggles and on what he observed to be "an extreme autistic aloneness" (p. 242). Asperger's interpretation suggests that autistic youth were hyperaware of their environment, in contrast to Kanner, who evokes the idea that in their "extreme autistic aloneness" autistic youth were indifferent to or unaware of their environment.

Although autism made its first appearance in the DSM's third edition (American Psychiatric Association, 1980), in later editions criteria became increasingly comprehensive and refined. Characteristics consistently outlined in the DSM criteria for autism-spectrum classifications match Kanner's and Asperger's observations. Broadly, the DSM describes autism as "qualitative impairment in social interaction," which includes characteristics such as communication impairments and restricted, repetitive, and stereotyped patterns of behavior, interests, and activities. Suggesting a sense of rigidity and a void of inventiveness and spontaneity, the DSM language echoes Kanner's primarily deficit orientation and seems to describe a population that bears a stronger semblance to robots than to people. In doing so, that language contributes to a rift between autism and humanity. This observation echoes a sentiment of autism activist Amanda Baggs (2007), who does not use conventional speech to communicate. She observes that because of her unusual style of language, she often is regarded as a nonperson.

The idea that autistic people have a limited ability to imagine and create emerges from the general concept that they are socially impaired, are unable to form fresh interpretations and ideas, and instead repeat hackneyed, inflexible patterns of behavior. One does not come away from reading the DSM criteria with the idea that autistic people often express elements of both the ability to imagine and create, as well as an inclination toward routine actions. In this way, the DSM veers from Asperger's overall constructive, balanced perspective.

The latest iteration of the DSM (DSM-5, American Psychiatric Association, 2013), like the earlier editions, articulates various qualities of social deficit necessary to justify a diagnosis of autism spectrum disorder (ASD).

In renaming the category ASD, the DSM-5 has modified its categorization of autism labels, eliminating once-distinct classifications such as Asperger syndrome and pervasive developmental disorder-not otherwise specified (PDD-NOS). This change was made in favor of collapsing the categories into one broad class of "disorders." Distinctions between positions on the spectrum are noted with specifiers, which state the intensity of qualities related to social difficulty, such as a sense of rigidity and the need for routine.

Shifting Attitudes Toward Autism

Despite the changes in defining autism demonstrated in different iterations of the DSM, qualities related to social development and ability have been mainstays. Historically, AS has been an identifier for those who experience social difficulties but use speech with facility. Classic autism, on the other hand, has been a descriptor for those who experience social difficulties and a lack of facility with speech. Changes to the various autism-spectrum classifications have reflected new knowledge and, recently, changing cultural landscapes. Over the years, distinct autism classifications have had significant demographic and cultural implications. For instance, while it does not elaborate on the reasoning for the bias, the DSM-5 Neurodevelopmental Disorders Workgroup notes that the shift to using ASD as a broad category came about in part due to the realization that AS was a classification overwhelmingly given to White, relatively affluent males. The PDD-NOS classification, on the other hand, historically has been given more often to non-Whites and members of poorer socioeconomic groups (W. E. Kaufman, 2012).

Interestingly, Autism Consortium, an autism cure-focused organization, posted on its website a symposium outline by W. E. Kaufman (2012), who is a member of the DSM-5 Workgroup. Detailing the changes contained within the DSM-5, the outline notes that in reworking the ASD classification, the Workgroup consulted with autism advocacy groups, and the vast majority reportedly approved of the change. In a piece written by Kapp and Ne'eman (2012) of Autism Self Advocacy Network (ASAN), the authors (both autistic) note that while there are select areas of the new classification criteria that they deem problematic, overall the change signifies "a positive development" (p. 2). It is striking that an organization focused on a cure for autism would post a document that reflected consultation with autism advocacy groups, although it contains comprehensive information. If the voices of advocates serve a distinct role in the reshaping of DSM language and criteria, it seems that Autism Consortium would be faced with some crucial questions: Does autism offer perspectives that neurotypicals can learn from and ways of being that can enrich the world socially and culturally? Or is autism in need of cure and eradication? This tension suggests that as the voices of autistic people continue to make their way into the broad culture, organizations that traditionally have positioned themselves as cure-oriented will benefit from integrating current ideas in the process of re-evaluating their stance and founding beliefs.

While the DSM-5 Workgroup reports that they failed to gain the support of one advocacy group, the act of consulting with and gaining the approval of many autism advocacy groups acknowledges the force and strength of these groups in shaping meanings of autism. The APA's regard for cultural, demographic, and advocacy-group response suggests a move toward integrating a more complex array of considerations and perspectives in making changes to the DSM criteria, at least for autism. This is a significant move in a process that impacts a vast number of people.

Contesting the Theory of Mind

Descriptors originating from DSM criteria, such as "inflexible," "restricted," "stereotyped," and "repetitive," are recursive in research literature on autism and contribute to the sense that autistic people have limitations in imaginative and creative abilities. A once-prominent idea that has been widely contested is that autistic people lack a theory of mind (ToM), which is the ability to take the perspective of others.

First applied to autism by psychologist Baron-Cohen and colleagues Leslie and Frith (1985), the theory holds that autistic people experience difficulties in social, emotional, and communicative areas due to a "core" deficit, the ability to understand the feelings and perspectives of others. The authors cite their study, in which 80% of autistic children failed a False Belief Task, a tool used to determine one's ability to take the perspective of another person. In contrast, 14% of children with Down syndrome and 15% of typically developing children failed the test. The task involves an illustration scenario showcasing two girls, Sally and Anne, as well as a basket, a box, and a marble. Sally places the marble in the basket when she decides to go outside to play. While Sally is out, Anne comes in and moves the marble from the basket to the box and then leaves. Sally then returns to the room. When asked where Sally will look to find the marble, children guess either the basket or the box. In the Baron-Cohen and colleagues study, 80% of the autistic youth responded that Sally would look in the box for the marble. The authors reasoned that the youths' failing to understand that Sally would look where she left the marble was due to their inability to understand Sally's perspective. It appears that the majority of autistic youth in the study used the information they acquired in observing Anne's actions and pointed to where the marble truly was as opposed to where Sally would think the marble was, based on where she left it before going outside. As a result of these findings, the authors concluded that there is concrete reason to believe that autistic youth have impaired abilities to take the perspective of others.

There are, of course, many likely alternative explanations for the participants giving the responses they gave. Here are a few possibilities that come to mind. It could be that rather than failing to understand Sally's perspective, the youth who did not pass the test were instead attending intensely to the full set of information they had acquired in the task. Perhaps once they had the full range of information at their disposal, it was difficult for them to go back to that discrete piece of information about Sally putting the marble in the basket before heading outside. Perhaps they understood Sally's perspective but chose to report what they knew to be true. Perhaps a regard for "truth" overshadowed Sally's perspective. Perhaps there was something about the question that made retrieval of pertinent information difficult. Perhaps if the situation had been real, taking place in a familiar context such as a classroom with trusted peers, the participants' responses might have been different. To conclude that autistic people lack a ToM based on a False Belief Task is a huge leap that overstates the importance and relevance of the test to authentic, real-life circumstances.

It has been argued that ToM shapes the way autistic people behave in diverse contexts, particularly those that require nuanced agility in reading the social atmosphere and responding according to rules and expectations deemed appropriate by the majority (neurotypical) culture. As I discuss in the coming chapters, the ways that autistic people process information, navigate personal relationships, and negotiate daily life provide evidence of their ability to understand that others have minds separate from their own.

In his book *The Reason I Jump*, Naoki Higashida (2013) attends to the way that others view him, and the structure of his book follows the observations others have made of him. Questions such as, "Why do you move your arms and legs about in that awkward way?" (p. 52) and, "Why do you memorize train tables and calendars?" (p. 79) serve as titles for his concise chapters, in which he responds to the queries. Likewise, in a now-classic piece, "Don't Mourn for Us," autistic writer Jim Sinclair (1993) contends, "When parents say 'I wish my child did not have autism', what they are really saying is 'I wish the autistic child I have did not exist, and I had a different (non-autistic) child instead'" (p. 1). Clearly, Sinclair's insights indicate that he conceives of some parents' thoughts about raising autistic children. Xu's (2012) description of autistic professor Melanie Yergeau's job interview highlights Yergeau's ability to take others' states of mind into account. During the interview, Yergeau made the decision to sit on her hands in order to mask her tendency to move her hands in a repetitive pattern (commonly referred to as stimming, an abbreviation of self-stimulatory behavior, which many autistic people experience). Had she not been able to imagine how the interviewer might judge her, Yergeau would not have bothered to try to curb her movements by sitting on her hands. These examples, as well as others I present later in this book, demonstrate that autistic individuals' insights and actions very frequently have the effect of refuting the ToM argument.

A STRENGTHS-BASED UNDERSTANDING OF AUTISM

Disability Studies and neurodiversity perspectives support an understanding of autistic people in terms of strengths and abilities. While understanding autism as indicative of strength is a critical feature of this book, so too is the idea that autistic strengths can contribute to the enrichment of society. DS and neurodiversity perspectives are compatible in that they challenge prevailing beliefs about disability and offer new ways of understanding a range of human experience.

Disability Studies

Work in DS is far-reaching and is represented in disciplines such as literature, history, archaeology, and education (see Wappett & Arndt, 2013). Despite differences these disciplines may represent, DS research shares the common goal of looking at disability in ways that challenge prevailing beliefs and attitudes. As a field of inquiry, DS came about in response to disability research that overwhelmingly reflected a deficit-oriented, medical-model perspective that situated the locus of disability within the individual. Disability, in this interpretation, was a deficit to be treated, overcome, or compensated for. DS scholarship, in contrast, has worked collectively within a social model of disability, focusing on external forces that contribute to disabling experiences. Research that highlights the complexity of disabled experiences, often by including the perspectives of people with disabilities, has contributed to interpretations of disability that are more holistic than those found in traditional, deficit-oriented research. DS work brings to light the ways that societal structures and attitudes favor the able-bodied "norm." This "norm" can contribute to numerous difficulties associated with navigating the world. A classic example is how a wheelchair user cannot navigate the streets with the ease that walking people do, if curb cuts are only sporadically installed on street corners. Likewise, an autistic person who is sensitive to certain sounds may have trouble concentrating during class if the lights on the ceiling are emitting a buzz. DS scholars commonly explore alternative ways to promote access to full societal participation for people with disabilities. Curb cuts, as it turns out, benefit a range of people besides wheelchair users, including people pushing children in strollers and those using dollies to cart heavy loads. Installing noise-free light fixtures helps a great range of people maintain focus, not just autistic students.

The idea that features of the environment can be designed to be useful and beneficial to a wide range of people across their life span is central to Universal Design (UD) principles and is compatible with DS work. For DS scholars, a key goal is to reconstruct the term "norm" and to question its validity and relevance to the full spectrum of humanity. DS scholars work to stretch, expand, and turn the idea of "normal" on its head, in order to represent a greater number of people and experiences.

In more recent years, some DS researchers have begun to bring attention to the very real ways physical features of impairment impact lives (e.g., Riddle, 2013). This vein of scholarship highlights how some physical elements of impairment, such as pain, exist regardless of societal attitudes and structures, and are integral features of life for many people. As DS scholarship evolves, it is clear that work in this tradition of inquiry is consistently concerned with an improved quality of life for people with disabilities. Uniting DS scholarship is the spirit of moving forward, toward more inclusive and equitable models of human experience and expression.

One powerful way that DS scholarship aims to challenge prevailing beliefs is to forefront views of people with disabilities. In the process of listening to the voices of those who are most intimately familiar with the experience of a disability, counter narratives often are revealed. That is, when people with disabilities describe their lives and experiences, they tend to speak holistically, not focusing uniquely on struggles, but also exposing areas of strength, capacity, and ability. These narratives often counter the types of information revealed in research that reflects traditional medical-model perspectives. In this book, the voices of autistic people are central, and, in alignment with DS goals, prevailing beliefs about the relationship between autism and creativity are challenged. The insights of autistic people are critical in evoking fresh interpretations that parallel autism with creative ability.

Neurodiversity

Regarding autistic people as members of a humanity that is neurodiverse parallels a commitment to DS inquiry. Neurodiversity refers to the way that one's neurological wiring (as manifested in a variety of ways, autism among them) influences one's way of experiencing and perceiving the world. The neurodiversity perspective holds that autism and other neurological ways of being that differ from neurotypicality are not lesser ways of being. For the autism self-advocacy group ASAN, aligning with the neurodiversity stance means accepting the reality that human beings have neurological differences and that those differences can manifest in diverse ways of being and influence one's perceptions and experiences (ASAN, 2015b). Autism, ASAN (2015a) notes, is in part characterized by sensitivity to features such as light, sound, and textures. Many autistic people report experiencing strong reactions to sensory stimuli, and the neurological basis for high reactivity to sensory stimuli is well supported in research. In her book on extroversion and introversion, Cain (2012) discusses psychologist Jerome Kagan's research on the different ways that infants responded to various sensory stimuli and how these responses foreshadowed their future temperaments (Kagan & Snidman, 2004). Some of the infants in the study reacted very strongly, by crying and pumping fists, to stimuli such as loud sounds (e.g., balloons popping) and unpleasant smells (for instance, cotton balls soaked in alcohol). Other babies had very relaxed reactions to these stimuli and showed little physical response. While presenting the babies with the various stimuli, Kagan's team looked at bodily features influenced by the nervous system (in particular, the part of the brain called the amygdala), such as the babies' heart rates and blood pressure. They found that the babies who showed the strongest reactions to the stimuli likewise evidenced more activity in the amygdala and showed, for example, higher heart rates than the babies who responded to the stimuli in more relaxed ways. Longitudinal follow-ups affirmed that those who were highly reactive as infants grew up to be adolescents who were more careful, quieter, and generally more leery of novelty than their less-reactive peers. Those who showed low reactivity to the stimuli as infants grew up to be adolescents who were more relaxed, socially confident, and generally less fearful of people and novel social situations than their high-reactive peers. In their work, Kagan and his team compellingly point to the ways that neurological wiring plays a significant role in the way one experiences and perceives the world.

Neurodiversity came about as a rebuttal to the conception that, in part due to neurological wiring that differs from that of most people (neurotypicality), autism is indicative of deficit and often is described in terms of the potential for recovery and cure (such as in Insel, 2007). Those who align with the neurodiversity stance have highlighted many representations of autism that counter prevailing myths. One such myth equates a lack of speech with a lack of intelligence. Another myth is that autistic people prefer solitude to community. Interestingly, the Internet has given autistic people an especially conducive form through which to communicate. For those who do not use speech, typing can be a preferred form of communication. Even for those who do speak, there are often benefits, such as lessened anxiety, to typing one's thoughts as opposed to saying them to a person directly. Email, YouTube, and online communities therefore have become rich resources for autistic people to gather and share thoughts and ideas in a way that supports and affirms their strengths. The neurodiversity movement maintains its momentum through the driving force of autistic self-advocates and their allies, who directly reject the goals of popular autism organizations that rally to cure and eradicate autism. Instead, the neurodiverse community, such as that represented in ASAN, understands autism to be an identity feature they do not wish to erase. Members often highlight how autism is a valuable place from which to perceive and experience life. A focus on difference of experience as opposed to deficit of experience reframes autism as a way of being that has its benefits and its difficulties. The same, of course, is true for any way of being. Many outspoken, well-known autistic people, such as White House council member Ari Ne'eman, scholar Melanie Yergeau, poet Tito Mukhopadhyay, and activist Amanda Baggs, align with a neurodiversity stance. Similarly, several scholars, such as Winter-Messiers (2007), Biklen (2005), Savarese (2010), and Rosqvist (2012), have contributed powerful work that presumes the competence (Biklen & Burke, 2006) of autistic people and evidences a neurodiversity perspective.

SPECIAL INTERESTS, CREATIVITY, AND IDENTITY FORMATION

Because autistic students often engage the world in different ways than do their neurotypical peers, it is important to figure out how their experiences can be meaningfully enfolded into school-based learning. Recognizing creativity as a process in which autistic youth do engage is crucial when considering the role that creativity plays in the evolution of self-concept. In research at the intersection of autism and schooling, there is an overwhelming focus on helping autistic students overcome or compensate for supposed social impairments. This focus can lead to educational opportunities that are qualitatively less rich than those of their neurotypical peers (see Osler & Osler, 2002).

Educational experiences that are watered down or separate, as exemplified in self-contained classrooms, send the message that autistic youth do not fit in with their neurotypical peers or within the structure of general education classrooms. This negative message, in turn, can contribute to a sense of stigma in these youth and work against the cultivation of healthy identities (i.e., self-concepts that include facets of competence and strength alongside areas of struggle and vulnerability). Holding negative perceptions of self, autistic students are often vulnerable to depression, anxiety, and social isolation (Carrington & Graham, 2001; Carrington, Templeton, & Papinczak, 2003). Furthermore, many autistic youth, who often communicate and behave in unconventional ways, are targets for bullying (Hay & Winn, 2005; Humphrey & Lewis, 2008).

The implications for cultivating a healthy identity are both immediate and far-reaching. Day-to-day experiences that include positive interactions with others can stave off feelings of self-doubt or a lack of belonging. Over time, school experiences that include positive interactions with others, especially peers, can cultivate a sense of community and the idea that one has valuable contributions to make to that community. The knowledge that one has unique attributes that can enrich a community can carry a youth into adulthood with the sense that he or she can participate meaningfully in culture and society.

An important way to foster a sense of inclusiveness in classrooms and schools is to acknowledge and develop students' individual strengths, which collectively can bolster the entire community. For autistic students, it can be particularly helpful to reference areas of interest or intense focus, since for many of these youth, these interests can be deeply intertwined with their sense of identity. Winter-Messiers (2007) aligns the cultivation of healthy identities in youth with AS with their ability to tap special interest areas in school-based endeavors. She underscores the importance of this alignment, noting that if students are not allowed to engage their special interests in school, they in fact are leaving "themselves at home" (p. 149). Winter-Messiers aptly observes that through the integration of special interests, learning becomes meaningful and less wrought with struggle for autistic students.

Implications for encouraging autistic students' interests thus include affirming their place in a diverse community of peers and supporting their development of a healthy sense of self. Recognizing and promoting creative thinking likewise can support the evolution of one's unique personality. Alluding to the way creativity acts as a change agent that alters one's "psychic development," Ghiselin (1985, p. 4) asserts creativity's transformative power. In contrast, research that assumes autistic students' inflexibility in thinking, and warns of their preoccupation with special interest areas, can work against these students' creative development. This avenue of research intimates that such intense interests distract students from engaging in school in acceptable ways. However, special interest areas represent a wellspring of opportunity to construct learning experiences that will engage autistic youth, help them develop creatively, and give teachers a sense of how these students process, think, communicate, and learn. In order for autistic students to be recognized for their creative ability, it is essential to regard their interests as more than mere preoccupations. The idea that special interests are well worth paying attention to in terms of enhancing classroom engagement for autistic students has been solidly documented (e.g., Furniss, 2009; Kluth, 2003; Winter-Messiers, 2007). However, the notion that special interests can both inspire creative engagement and provide evidence of creative capacity merits the deeper consideration of the chapters that follow.

CREATIVITY AS A HUMAN COMMONALITY

Since at least the middle of the 20th century, *creativity* has been an umbrella term subsuming a number of qualities, including, according to Ogata (2013), "inventiveness, problem solving, insightfulness, originality, and discovery of personal potential" (p. 1). In this definition, creativity is situated as an inclusive quality that all people have experience with. It likewise is interpreted to be a quality that thrives on novelty of expression and diversity of perspectives. So while creativity is broadly understood as common, it is striking how the tenor changes, within both popular media and scholarship, when the conversation turns to autistic people. The lack of a parallel between autism and creativity is particularly striking when considering the unconventional, novel ways in which autistic people often engage and experience the world. Indeed, Asperger (1944/1991) observed and made frequent reference to the novelty with which autistic youth perceive the world, at one point writing that "autistic children have the ability to see things and events around them from a new point of view, which often shows surprising maturity" (p. 71).

Many autistic people have disrupted common conceptions about autism by contributing narratives that highlight their abilities. A web search for Amanda Baggs, for instance, will lead one to a 2007 YouTube video titled *In My Language*, which demonstrates her articulate thinking through an unconventional communication style that combines vocalizations, interaction with textural elements, and bodily movements with typing. In "Don't Mourn for Us," Sinclair (1993) likewise reveals a clear, thoughtful, provocative mind. Acts such as these, as well as everyday acts by less well-known autistic people, indicate enormous creative and imaginative capacity.

In the scholarly literature on autism and schooling, a focus on what autistic students apparently cannot do has overshadowed the multitude of abilities that educators and family members have observed these students to demonstrate on a regular basis. While the contributions of high-profile autistic people such as Baggs and Sinclair suggest high levels of creativity, creative ability likewise is regularly apparent in classrooms and schools. This ability is evident among all students, including autistic youth, in the tapping of one's experiential knowledge in the process of constructing new knowledge, referencing one's interests to express oneself and connect with others, and engaging challenge in efforts to grow beyond one's current capacities. In the coming chapters, characteristics such as these are highlighted as evidence of creative and imaginative abilities. Recognizing that these qualities indicate creative ability is an important step in acknowledging that autistic people participate in a process so fundamental to being human.

While some scholars have looked at the creativity of autistic people who have showed extraordinary creative contribution (e.g., Fitzgerald, 2005; Happe & Frith, 2010), it is rare to find scholarly work that regards the more everyday experiences of autistic people as indicative of creativity. Although anecdotes about the everyday creative and imaginative abilities in autistic people can be found in informal spaces such as Internet forums (e.g., autism.about.com/b/2008/09/09/do-people-with-autism-lack-imagination.htm), education researchers have given little attention to the topic.

As an extension, there is an absence of work that focuses on the skills and abilities that are catalyzed in the process of autistic individuals' creative engagement. It is typically more common to find work citing the many ways that autistic people are rigid, stereotyped in their actions and mannerisms, and mired in singular worlds of their personal obsessions (where "obsessions" take on a pessimistic connotation). These interpretations infer a sense of doubt: How can a person cultivate imagination and creativity if he or she is rigid and sticks to stereotypic representations of reality? In light of this, it is reassuring to visit the ideas of creativity theorists who stress the inclusivity of creative experience. As referenced at the opening of this chapter, Carter's (2004) dictum, "Creativity is not simply a property of exceptional people but an exceptional property of all people" (p. 13), supports the idea that autistic people, as members of humanity, cannot be exempt from this attribute.

Ghiselin (1985) similarly considers creativity a human process "of change, of development, of evolution, in the organization of subjective life" (p. 2). Likewise, in their discussion of varying degrees and types of creative manifestation, J. C. Kaufman and Beghetto (2009) note the importance of gaining greater insight into the everyday creativity expressed by students in school contexts. They posit that too often acts of creativity are overlooked due to educators' restricted vision of what creativity "means" or how it might appear in nuanced ways (p. 4). They evoke Vygotsky (1967/2004), who contended,

> Any human act that gives rise to something new is referred to as a creative act, regardless of whether what is created is a physical object or some mental or emotional construct that lives within the person that created it, and is known only to him. (p. 7)

Rather than a process reserved for those deemed "gifted" or "talented," typically in the arts, Vygotsky regards creativity as a process that is enacted within the midst of negotiating life. His observation implies that everyday creative negotiations occur in school-based learning, in socialization, and in solitary experiences. Vygotsky's sentiment reaches across status of ability and considers the process of creativity as inseparable from the experience of being human.

TOWARD RECOGNITION, ACKNOWLEDGMENT, AND SUPPORT OF CREATIVITY IN AUTISTIC STUDENTS

Disrupting the dominant conception of autism as indicative of rigidity and impairment in creative and imaginative ability expands understandings of what it means to be autistic. The disruption likewise bears implications for improving a sense of inclusiveness and community in classrooms and schools. A shift toward understanding that autistic characteristics represent difference as opposed to deficit can expand class-wide expectations of a range of behavioral dispositions. When students expect that diversity exists among members of any group, they are in a position to learn from those classmates who represent difference. They are further prepared to understand that human expression comes in many forms and that neurotypical ways of being only partially represent human variation. Autistic students, when treated as valuable members of a classroom and school community, can learn about navigating the social world in authentic contexts with their peers.

Viewing autistic students as creatively able and competent also has important implications for scholarship and practice, which traditionally have focused on discrete strategies for remediating behaviors that are deemed to be socially inappropriate. Historically, the quality of educational experiences aimed at autistic students have included behavior–reward models such as applied behavioral analysis (Leblanc, Richardson, & McIntosh, 2005) and step-by-step instructions on how to navigate a novel social situation or encounter, such as is typified in the SODA (Stop, Observe, Deliberate, Act) strategy (Bock, 2001). Social stories, popularized by Gray (1995), are likewise a common type of intervention suggested for autistic students. The value of approaches such as SODA and social stories is in helping students work through potentially overwhelming situations with a clear sense of what actions they need to take. These strategies have likely been quite helpful to many people, although they do have their limits. For one, lock-step approaches can be isolating, particularly if they are used only with autistic students. These approaches likewise pay little heed to the ways that autistic students do, in many instances and in their own ways, successfully navigate social situations in authentic relationship with others. These interventions, aimed to help autistic students reach more normative (neurotypical) ways of navigating the social world, may discredit autistic students' styles of communicating as ineffective or inappropriate. While there are times when autistic students may benefit from these types of interventions, they bear more relevance if students have a stake in deciding what strategies will help them navigate the social world with better confidence and reliability. If, for example, an autistic student deems social stories to be helpful, then incorporating these strategies into curricular learning can be an empowering tool. However, choosing to predominately use these types of intervention without the consultation or consideration of the student and his or her caretakers presents a missed opportunity for the student to advocate on behalf of him- or herself. Furthermore, while the assumption may be that autistic students need such intervention, many other students also may benefit from using social navigation tools. In a diverse learning community, these types of interventions can be offered to all students and incorporated into class-wide curricular experiences. Offering these tools on a broad basis may alleviate the tension that can arise when one group (i.e., autistic students) is offered a remedial modification while the other students go on to do more "typical," subject-specific curricular activities.

In that the use of social intervention strategies can be isolating, they do little to help build community within classroom contexts. Rather, the strategies place the burden on the autistic student to assimilate to normative standards of social behavior. A move toward acknowledging that all students are creatively able is one way to construct learning communities that are egalitarian and inclusive. Since creativity is a quality that invites difference and novelty, it is an opportune portal through which various expressive representations can be understood as valuable and acceptable. An autistic student can feel validated that his or her communication or social navigation style is acceptable in an environment that expects difference. In such an environment, neurotypical class members come to understand that there are numerous ways of engaging the social world, and autistic students can broaden neurotypical students' perspectives in this regard.

Because more holistic understandings of autism can support the cultivation of healthy identities of autistic youth, there is a need for narratives of autism that include demonstrations of creative ability. Of equal importance to aligning autism with creative ability is the potential for improved classroom and school-based practices. Acknowledging the creative ability of autistic students is an act of inclusiveness and strengthens a sense of community and commonality among all students, within classrooms and schoolwide. Providing ample opportunity for autistic students, along with their peers, to engage in creative processes can give educators a chance to see qualities that perhaps had gone unnoticed before. Educators can use these observations to design curricular experiences that reflect and integrate students' interests, propensities, goals, and dreams.

The coming chapters focus on ways that autistic people express themselves creatively through thinking, action, conversation, autobiography, fiction writing, poetry, painting, illustration, musical performance, and acting. These individuals demonstrate how creative expression can support a number of skills, abilities, and qualities that enrich their lives in numerous ways. Further, they show how negotiating life in and out of school constitutes the sort of everyday creativity that all people engage in on a regular basis.

In the following chapters, I align autism with creativity and demonstrate how this alignment can cultivate ideas for helping autistic students develop their creative potentials.

CHAPTER 2

Aligning Autism and Creativity Through Scholarship and Autobiography

It's time to expand my abilities and let my disabilities live in peace.

—Ido Kedar (2012)

Autism's relationship to creativity is complex—conflicted, confusing, and often contradictory. By some accounts, autism signifies an extraordinary way of being parallel to genius. By most others, and as discussed in the previous chapter, autism signifies impairment in abilities to imagine and create. The former of these descriptions points to select autistic individuals as surpassing most other people creatively, and the latter suggests that most often autistic people are far less creatively able than most other people. These hierarchical divisions make it difficult to understand autistic people as capable of the sort of imaginative and creative processes in which all people engage on a regular basis. With the exception of references to extraordinary feats of creativity by autistic individuals, an alignment between creativity and autism is not commonly made.

When creativity is discussed with regard to autism, it frequently is couched, as in Craig and Baron-Cohen (1999), to be "reality-based" (p. 319). This type of creativity is positioned as a limited form or less indicative of imagination. Yet interestingly, contemporary creativity research frequently asserts that creativity most certainly is tied to problems or obstacles presented in everyday life, as well as reflective of one's personal interests and abilities. Contrary to common beliefs, creativity scholars note that creative ideas do not materialize out of thin air (Beghetto & Kaufman, 2010). Rather, they are very much tied to one's lived experiences and needs.

Evidence that creative thinking and ability are regular attributes of autistic people can be found in some autism scholarship and quite abundantly in autism autobiography. These strands of work highlight qualities such as innovation in thought, a sense of humor, a drive to problem-solve, and a wish to contribute insight about autistic life experience that can help other autistic people. In doing so, they disrupt dominant narratives that parallel autism with either savant-like ability or an impaired ability to imagine and create. The focus, then, is shifted to the constructive ways autistic people are working toward a more equitable future for others who share aspects of their realities.

In this chapter, I begin by exploring how autism at times is framed as synonymous with extraordinary ability and share how this framing contradicts the notion of an impaired ability to imagine and create. I draw attention to the way extraordinary accounts cultivate misleading representations of autism, and emphasize instead the need for the cultivation of everyday forms of creativity in classrooms and schools. I then further this discussion with insights culled from select autism scholarship and autism autobiography, demonstrating an alignment of autism with creative, imaginative ability. Throughout, I reference and weave relevant ideas from creativity scholarship in efforts to demonstrate how characteristics of autism and creativity can support and build on one another.

ACCOUNTS OF THE EXTRAORDINARY

Discussions about autistic people's lack of a ToM, and thus the ability to imagine and create, often are complicated by the way autistic people commonly are positioned as intellectually capable, with "undoubted special abilities" (Wing, 2005, p. 200), and as gifted (e.g., Bianco, Carothers, & Smiley, 2009; Henderson, 2001; Little, 2002). Similarly, literature and popular media often capitalize on a widely held assumption: that many autistic people are somehow extraordinarily gifted, intellectually bright, or talented. Such narratives point to exemplars such as Temple Grandin, who is an accomplished scientist, inventor, and writer. Or to youth who have shown an unusual ability to draw or calculate mathematical problems, phonetically read at a very young age, or recite from memory geographical data, train schedules, and so forth. Others reference historical geniuses such as Michelangelo, Einstein, and Mozart, who some speculate were autistic given their social awkwardness and heightened ability to focus. Consequently, these narratives, in their allowance of characteristics associated with autism that are positive or even desired given society's reverence for intellectual ability, at times frame autism as hierarchically superior to other ways of being. Narratives of autism as extraordinary certainly have acted as a foil to prevailing beliefs about autism as a metaphor for inability and deficit. In doing so, they have pushed the conception of autism to new places and introduced the idea that autism indeed can be indicative of desirable ways of being.

Big-C and little-c Creativity

Studies of extraordinary creativity among autistic savants (e.g., Happe & Frith, 2010), as well as analyses of historical figures that are posthumously speculated to have demonstrated traits associated with autism (e.g., Fitzgerald, 2004, 2005), are fairly common areas of research. These accounts represent what creativity scholars such as J. C. Kaufman and Beghetto (2009) often refer to as exemplars of Big-C creativity, and focus on those few people who reach an elite status of success that often is discussed alongside descriptors such as "genius" and "legacy." Big-C creativity, as contrasted to little-c creativity, "consists of clear-cut, eminent creative contributions" (p. 2). Some creativity theorists note that Big-C creativity is distinguished from little-c forms in that it changes culture or history in some remarkable way (e.g., Csikszentmihalyi, 1996). In fact, creativity scholar Boden (2004) refers to this form of creativity as Historical (or "H") creativity.

While the Big-C/little-c framework plays a prominent role in creativity scholarship, it is not entirely clear who originated the model. Merrotsy (2013) addresses the enigma in a commentary where he attempts to trace the roots of Big-C/little-c. He notes that in 1953 creativity theorist Stein wrote about distinctions among creativity types, which formed the basic framework for Big-C/little-c. Merrotsy further found that Luckenbach (1986) was likely the first to denote Big-C/little-c by name in print.

Until approximately 25 years ago, Big-C creativity was the predominant focus of research to the broad exclusion of less brilliant forms of creativity (Merrotsy, 2013). Everyday, or little-c, creativity has become a frequently researched construct only in recent decades, as a growing interest in creative processes (as opposed to products, which typically have been the foci of Big-C research) has taken hold (Miller, Lambert, & Speirs Neumeister, 2012). A shift toward researching little-c processes over Big-C products has had direct implications for classrooms and schools. Better understanding of the ways people engage creative processes in everyday life can give educators insight into ways to encourage all students' creative potentials.

Contextual Features and Supports for Creative Development

Scratching beneath the surface of "extraordinary" autism narratives, such as those focusing on savants, it becomes clear that such qualities as "talent" and "giftedness" most often are revealed through supportive contextual features. These features include ample opportunity to engage interests, access to high-quality schooling, parental interest in a child's success, and communities that value these constructs. These types of conditions for success likewise can be applied to educational contexts. As I discuss later in this chapter, Grandin (2006), for example, reports a steady stream of personal support from her mother, select teachers, and friends who helped her navigate difficult social situations. She had people who advocated with her and on her behalf, believed in her abilities, and helped align her with people and communities that would support her strengths. Grandin's ability to achieve professional success was no accident. Rather, it was the result of consistent, thoughtful, constructive structures of support in her life, a life that was deemed valuable from the beginning.

Similarly, there are multiple factors at play in the evolution of a person or product that a culture deems "genius." Creativity researcher Csikszentmihalyi (1996) discusses in detail the confluences of factors that aligned for so much remarkable creativity to flourish in Renaissance Florence. There were several features present: public support for artistic contribution, an openness to diverse artistic interpretations, a renewed interest in antiquated ways of building structures, a desire to cultivate a city as beautiful as ancient Athens, as well as the philanthropic support of wealthy citizens to commission work. Without these features of support, artists such as Ghiberti and Brunelleschi would not have been in a position to take on their lifelong projects of the Florence Baptistery doors. Starting at age 21, Ghiberti spent 48 years constructing the north and east doors of the Florence Baptistery. This reality suggests that one's ability to focus for prolonged periods of time and on a singular interest are cultivated at least in part by the support and liberty one is given to express his or her creativity. The conditions of support play an enormous role in such clear-cut forms of success.

In terms of school-based application, Big-C contributions and extraordinary accounts of autistic experience have far less relevance for helping the majority of students (autistic and neurotypical) develop their creative potentials than do little-c forms of creativity. Despite their focus on rare instances of creativity, however, a major benefit of Big-C studies is that they highlight the fact that contextual supports can help people cultivate their creative potentials. This understanding is an integral step in constructing creative learning experiences for students in classrooms and schools.

If educators can build supports into school-based structures, autistic students, as well as other students, will be in better positions to succeed in cultivating their creative potentials. Creativity and education scholar Runco (2010) embraces the idea that all students have creative potential and supports educators' investment of energy into helping them cultivate these potentials. The payoff of doing so, he notes, will be much greater than focusing educational resources on students who already exhibit a high degree of creativity. Students who do not show high levels of creativity can improve their creative ability when given support to do so. Even when creativity is enhanced incrementally, he reasons, the cumulative effect is great since the majority of students fall outside of the category of exceptionally high creative ability. Students who demonstrate high levels of creativity, Runco notes, "require very little to maintain their already creative behavior and performances" (p. 240). The assumption is that these youth will create regardless of the presence or absence of external encouragement. Runco's observations point to the importance of shifting focus from encouraging the extraordinary to cultivating the everyday creative ability of most students—that is, to approach the cultivation of creativity within the classroom by attending to curricular adaptations that allow for all students to expand their repertoire of skills, regardless of whether they show strong creative impulses or abilities.

Where Extraordinary Misleads

Like the study of Big-C creativity, extraordinary narratives of autism can work against the idea that all people are creatively capable. At best, narratives that position autism as synonymous with extraordinary qualities add to the complexity of autism's meanings. At worst, they position autism as a hierarchically superior way of being or oversimplify and downplay difficult aspects of autism. Not all autistic people, for instance, equate with giftedness or talent their ability to focus intensely or attend to personal interests. Some consider these traits burdensome, at least in some contexts. Relatedly, qualities that in certain contexts represent positive attributes conversely can be the root of anxiety and distraction in others. Such was the case with Yergeau during the job interview mentioned in Chapter 1. While stimming typically seems to soothe a sense of feeling overwhelmed for Yergeau, it also can be a hindrance in circumstances where she would prefer not to stim. Similarly, Grandin (2006) describes how her ability to understand the world through logic benefits her career as a scientist in many ways. However, in order to navigate the personal aspects of her career, she has had to construct systems for relating to people socially, which requires attention to emotions as well. While Grandin does not naturally understand the world through an emotional lens, she does have strategies for attending to others' emotions through systems of logic. Context, as illuminated in these examples, plays a pivotal role in the way that characteristics associated with autism affect one's life in different ways.

While narratives of the extraordinary have interrupted the idea that autistic people lack intellectual competency, they simultaneously contribute to a narrative that equates autism with a way of being that is somehow difficult to relate to, or "enigmatic" (Frith, 2003). As applied to classrooms and schools, such conceptions are arguably of little use beyond disrupting common negative stereotypes of autism. Conceiving of autistic students as "extraordinary" by definition enforces a binary of ordinary (normal)/ beyond ordinary (abnormal). Being perceived as categorically "different," where difference is interpreted as deficit rather than an expected form of human variation, can work against these students' ability to find common ground with neurotypical peers. It also can cloud others' perceptions of these students' abilities and, as discussed in Chapter 1, take a toll on the evolving identities of autistic youth.

CREATIVE CAPACITY DEMONSTRATED THROUGH AUTISM SCHOLARSHIP

In light of the paucity of work that connects autism with the sort of creative resources that all people access on a regular basis, it is fruitful to mine scholarship that describes some of the ways that autistic people navigate life circumstances. This work illuminates how autistic people problem-solve issues that are relevant to their lives and personal circumstances. These studies are significant because they highlight how working with various constraints can promote effective, yet at times unconventional, solutions to problems.

The Strengths-Based Narrative of Hans Asperger

As the original voice in discussions about AS, pediatrician Hans Asperger discussed the youth with whom he worked in a way that balanced their difficulties with their abilities. His descriptions were written within a year (1944) of Kanner's (1943) descriptions of autism, and, as discussed in Chapter 1, each doctor described similar qualities in the patients with whom he worked. Asperger's interpretation of "abnormal" seems to evoke a constructive quality. Usually, "abnormal" evokes a pessimistic connotation, yet while Asperger (1944/1991) noted that in some cases his patients' social difficulties "overshadow everything else" (p. 37), he also observed his patients to have the potential to do well in several areas such as the arts and sciences. He demonstrated a sense of optimism, noting that although they may have profound difficulties, the youth "can fulfill their social role within the community, especially if they find understanding, love, and guidance" (p. 37). Significantly, Asperger offered insight as to how these youth might be supported to reach their creative potentials. He encouraged educational structures "where teachers would work with them rather than against them, building on their strengths and circumventing their weaknesses," and where students were "guided by their own special interests" (Frith, 2004, p. 673). One of the original voices to describe characteristics that came to be associated with ASD,

Asperger likewise appears to have contributed an original strengths-based narrative of the classification.

Responsive Expression to School-Based Problems

More recent scholarship also has aligned autism with resourceful problem-solving ability, as evidenced in the following examples.

Standing Up to Bullying. Hay and Winn (2005) discuss a circumstance where an everyday problem for many autistic youth, being bullied, spurred one student's spontaneous response. A young man with AS responded to a peer's disparaging remark in a way that while perhaps "inappropriate" by schools' estimation, nonetheless was nothing short of relevant. When his peer called him "mental" (p. 148), the young man with AS responded by putting the bully in a "head lock until he said sorry" (p. 148). Considering the reality that historically schools often have failed to manage and resolve bullying issues, and that many autistic students deal with being bullied on a routine basis, taking matters into one's own hands when faced with a bully can be understood as a resourceful attempt to resolve a serious problem. Reciprocating the schoolmate's hostility, the victim asserted his agency while sending the unmistakable message that he was willing to engage on par with his peer. On-the-spot thinking was a critical element in his ability to make his schoolmate consider backing off and thinking before attacking again.

Writing to Problem-Solve. Referencing another school-based incident, Osler and Osler (2002) demonstrate how novel expression of ideas can be powerfully represented in formal letter writing. In this work, Chay Osler, a high school student with AS, contributes his perspective in a letter he wrote to school officials regarding difficulties in school related to his seizures, AS, and bullying. In the work, Chay's aunt and coauthor, a professor of education, recounts a time when she helped advocate for Chay (with his mother) in response to his repeated exclusion from school. During his junior year in high school, Chay was excluded from school due to a series of seizures. School officials concluded that Chay's seizures posed problems that they did not have the resources to deal with. Excluded during a period of intense test preparation, he missed the opportunity to share resources with his peers that would have aided his readiness for test-taking. The act of exclusion prompted his family to meet with school officials about the relationship between the seizures and the stress experienced by Chay due to incessant bullying in school and a lack of academic support for challenges he faced in conjunction with AS. At his request, Chay participated in the meetings. One of the promises the authorities made to Chay was that he would be assigned a personal mentor to help him meet his educational goals. Yet over time, the promise, along with others, went unfulfilled, and Chay voiced his subsequent frustration.

Chay's requests were unfulfilled by school officials, who focused on the way Chay's supposed epilepsy (as it turned out, Chay's doctor said that his seizures were the result of stress rather than of epilepsy) posed an obstacle that hindered their ability to provide the resources to support Chay fully in school. Osler notes, "By medicalizing his 'problem,' the staff effectively absolve themselves of professional responsibility for his learning and welfare in school" (p. 52). A passionate literacy student with a propensity for writing (he reported to be working on a novel), Chay chose letter writing as a forum through which to present his thoughts to school authorities. In the letter, Chay provided details of the viewpoint that he previously had conveyed verbally during meetings. Writing gave Chay the opportunity to flesh out his ideas and to express his thoughts with a sense of depth and clarity. At one point, he wrote, "Excluding me from school because of seizures was, of course, very wrong . . . I should like decent, realistic, and sensible advice from my teachers" (p. 42). Chay further pointed out that telling him to ignore the bullies, as his teachers had been, was of no help to him. He highlights the crux of the problem he faces, asserting, "If the seizures were to stop the school would have no excuse to neglect me and I would be less stressed. On the other hand, they will not stop until the school can support me and enable me to be less stressed" (p. 42).

The act of writing gave Chay an opportunity to stand up to what he perceived to be numerous injustices. As a medium, formal letter writing allowed him to comprehensively and attentively express his views in a way that integrated real-life events with hoped-for outcomes. A plea for help in finding ways to alleviate his stress evidences his resourcefulness and attention to helping solve problems in concert with school professionals. In writing his letter, Chay constructed a piece that evidenced his ability to imagine a more just and inclusive schooling structure, where professionals would act as advocates in supporting his preparation for a future that would be more equitable than his present situation.

Connecting Through Inventive Mannerisms. Education researcher Linneman (2001) gives an account of the inventive mannerisms of Emily, a mostly nonverbal autistic girl about to enter kindergarten when the study began. Linneman highlights the expressive ways in which Emily communicated and connected with him over the course of 5 months, and again 4 years later. The study traces Linneman's tutorial sessions with Emily, as well as her development of computer skills, frequently through the program SuperPaint. Over their time together, Emily mastered several of the learning objectives that Linneman developed for her, including basic keyboard and mouse use; opening, closing, and creating files; working on a document; saving work; and so on. While Emily spoke very little during the time they worked together, Linneman documented her subtle expressive qualities that helped him forge a connection with her. At times, Emily would retreat to her mother's lap sucking her thumb or zone out watching a program on TV. Other times, though, Emily's movements and gestures revealed a unique manner of applying her new skills as well as her engagement and enjoyment of her work with Linneman. He shares, "Emily used her forearms, elbows, and really, her whole arm on the keyboard. Sometimes, she'd take her right hand and sweep her fingers over the keys and complete the movement with a flourish that ended with her hand aloft, excellently positioned for a high-five from me" (p. 127). He likewise noted how she clapped along to a Thelonius Monk song that played as the computer booted up and how, one time, she "arch[ed] her neck and shoulders and wave[d] her head back and forth like she [was] Stevie Wonder and reach[ed] her hand up for a high-five" (p. 129). In the absence of speech, attending to Emily's nonverbal, highly expressive cues allowed Linneman to gain insight into her sense of humor, her preferences, and her state of mind.

Over their time working together, Linneman engaged Emily in various linguistic practices: in dialogue about computer work, on telephone conversations, in teaching her to type out words and phrases, and through storytelling. While Emily's verbal skills developed over their months working together, Linneman consistently attended to the quality of her nonverbal expressive language. Emily's communication reflected a distinct sense of playfulness and desire to build friendship, as indicated in the high-fives she often prompted from Linneman. Linneman shared a time when he figured out that Emily was playing an indirect form of hide-and-seek with him. As she faced the TV, Linneman would fix his gaze on her reflection, and their eyes would meet on-screen. Linneman realized that Emily was playing with him because, as he noted, "When I would look, she would look away and laugh" (p. 131). Emily's creative use of movement and expression helped the two formulate a bond that lasted beyond the 5 months they worked together.

Four years later, when Emily was about to enter 4th grade, the two met up again. Linneman shares the dialogue they exchanged, which included various references to their past. Speaking elaborately now, Emily shared new discoveries she had learned on the computer, joked with Linneman about his being "a cool dude" (p. 181) because he wore a beaded necklace, and acknowledged how tired he must have been after having driven over an hour to see her that day. The two continued to share a strong rapport even 4 years later, and it seems plausible that a sense of mutual respect at the start laid the foundation for that sustained sense of trust. The mainly nonverbal devices that Emily initially used to communicate with Linneman were readily accepted, consistently acknowledged, and built upon to aid her development of verbal expression. This is not to say that Linneman did not encounter difficulty in the process of cultivating a relationship with Emily. He reported instances of frustration with Emily's mother, who intervened in efforts to manage her daughter's behavior during tutorial sessions. Linneman, in turn, pushed back, consistently but diplomatically demanding the space to develop a relationship with Emily on terms that worked for him and for her.

Creative Resistance

The theme of bucking outside forces, even those exerted by well-intended loved ones, is not foreign to narratives of autism. Biklen's book *Autism and the Myth of the Person Alone* (2005) showcases the work of a number of autistic coauthors, many of whom demonstrate creative "pushing back" in varying forms.

Gaining Independence. Biklen describes how one contributor, Alberto Frugone (2005), who types to communicate his thoughts, worked to gain independence in his daily life. Since Frugone relied upon his mother's assistance in aspects of daily living and functioning, he typically accompanied her on every errand she needed to do. Having grown tired of this routine in early adulthood, Frugone initiated a system that would allow him to stay behind while his mother did her errands out of the home. He first asked his mother if she could tape record herself yelling, "Help!" so that in the case of an emergency, Frugone could push the button and play his mother's plea for a neighbor to hear. His mother opposed the idea and felt that in a state of stress, he would be too flustered to carry out the task. But eventually the two settled on the compromise of a panic button that Frugone could push if she was out while he was home alone. In asserting a degree of independence, Frugone resisted established patterns. In the act of resistance to established norms and expectations, he relevantly and inventively addressed a problem he faced in his transition into adulthood.

Demonstrating Depth of Ideas. In another case, Biklen describes contributing author Lucy Blackman's (2005) arresting perspective on autism and access. He notes how Blackman, who also uses typing to communicate her thoughts, prompts him with direct frankness to explain why integration is beneficial for people with disabilities. When Biklen suggests that inclusion is important for students with disabilities to be understood as ordinary, Blackman presses him to provide a rationale for his point of view, which she regards as "idealistic" (Biklen, 2005, p. 53). She argues that normalizing disability threatens to erase important differences.

Blackman deems the evasion of differences related to autism as counterproductive to her educational and personal growth. She points to the need for educational (and presumably other) contexts that acknowledge and address her particular needs so that she can participate in a community of peers. Blackman's participatory style is nonconventional. For example, in reflecting on her college experiences, she discussed the need to walk the halls in order to process learning and stimuli, and to manage anxiety and excitement. Because she typed her responses and ideas, which was a slow process, she required far more time than most of her classmates to contribute responses during class discussions. Classmates needed to wait some time to receive her ideas. While these participatory forms are unusual and time-consuming, they are undoubtedly necessary for Blackman's ability to contribute her rich, astute thoughts and ideas to her educational community.

In written conversation with Biklen, Blackman also proposes turning disability from a problem, as it historically has been treated within schools, into a potential for profit. She explains that if somehow the integration (a.k.a. inclusion, mainstreaming) of disabled students could be aligned with economic profitability, then integration might become "popular" (Biklen, 2005, p. 54).

Interestingly, her ideas seem to play off those at the core of the social efficiency model of education, which has sustained dominance since the Industrial Revolution. The social efficiency model rests on the idea that for classrooms and schools to run smoothly, students must behave, respond, and participate in generally the same ways. They must be capable of and willing to adhere and conform to the conventions of classrooms and schools, which typically are structured around the transmission of ideas from teacher (the locus of authority) to students. Those who do comply learn in an environment that for the most part is controlled, managed, and relatively free of unpredictable interruption (e.g., from less conventional learners). Those who do not comply, who are aberrant or "misfits" (such as students with disabilities), are separated out, taken from the stream of an otherwise smooth running system, and given different treatment, curricula, expectations, and so forth. This structure, which is the basis for general education/special education, is assumed to most efficiently process students through the schooling system, and one effect is the inevitable tracking of students. Segregation of disabled and nondisabled students creates a divide that is very difficult to penetrate. How can peers of diverse abilities and ways of being learn to understand and accept one another when they are taught that they do not even belong in the classroom together?

Social efficiency relates to profit in terms of long-term human capital: At the end of the day, the reasoning goes, the socially efficient system presumably reveals the greatest educational "profit," with the majority of students gaining the benefits of the general education curricula. These students are envisioned to eventually become marketable citizens, who work at jobs and find occupations that create and contribute to a strong society and a thriving economic system. Blackman keenly observes that what is taken seriously in educational policy and practice is that which relates to social and economic profitability. If disability becomes a profitable enterprise, she notes, only then will people with disabilities stand a chance to truly "find acceptance" (Biklen, 2005, p. 53).

Blackman sees a need to both uphold differences and locate ways to work toward true acceptance of autistic people within societal structures. She cautions the threat of erasure of important differences if autistic people are understood as "ordinary." Her view seems to suggest the need for authentic integration with diverse peers that is built upon an expectation of difference. From Blackman's view, it would seem to follow that a movement from segregated learning environments to integrated learning environments would need to entail structural changes that implied an economic imperative. While the idea of applying a business model (profit-making) to (mostly) free public education is counterintuitive, Blackman's ideas can prompt a consideration of how to devise effective strategies for teaching diverse classes of students in more economically viable ways. This is a particularly relevant yet tenuous issue given the tight financial resources for public education in general. Many of the strategies discussed in Chapter 1, such as differentiation and structural modifications, come to mind. For instance, while often highly effective, collaborative team teaching requires two full-time salaried teachers within one classroom, which is expensive. Yet CTT models bear many benefits to classrooms and students, which makes finding ways to support the practice and to make it economically possible an important goal. Blackman's insights illuminate an instance of relying on familiar models (social efficiency, capitalism) to construct a novel interpretation that addresses a relevant, contemporary, pressing problem. Blackman's thoughts were so compelling to Biklen (2005) that he credits her with the beginning of his alignment with a "presuming competence" stance. This stance, he notes, deems "the person labeled autistic as a thinking, feeling person" (p. 73).

Biklen's collaboration certainly highlights the thinking, feeling capacities of his autistic coauthors. Some of the authors demonstrate these qualities with creative use of language. As I share in detail in the next chapter, Tito Mukhopadhyay, for instance, communicates with rich metaphor, and his poetry tells of what autism means to him: how it informs his perceptions, his feelings, and his sense of connectedness with other things. Mukhopadhyay's metaphorically rich use of language is a topic that Ralph Savarese, writer, scholar, and father of a nonverbal autistic son, likewise takes up.

Autism as a Vantage Point for Understanding Creativity

In an essay exploring the relationship between linguistic expression and what commonly is deemed "low-functioning" autism, Savarese (2010) observes that "some of the strangeness of autistic writing, but also its beauty, originates in different operational metaphors that spatially situate (or fail to situate) the person" (p. 279). This sentiment speaks to the importance of expanding conceptions of what it means to be autistic. It also positions autism as an opportunity to inform a greater understanding of human experience and variation. On one level, it suggests the existence of a relationship between autism and creative ability, as manifested in the use of unique metaphoric expression. On another level, it alludes to autism's distinct place in the evolving understanding of creative processes, as rooted in one's perception of his or her relationship to the physical space inhabited. Finally, the sentiment connects autistic expression to beauty, a bold interruption to the way autism typically is portrayed in research and popular media alike. The significance of Savarese's observation resides in its affirmation of autism as a source from which to expand understandings of what it means to be human. Savarese's statement challenges contemporary notions of autism and its relationship to creativity and imagination.

Experiencing the Body in Space. Savarese (2010) discusses how Mukhopadhyay's use of language is highly reflective of the way he experiences his body on a sensory level. Pointing to the way that prepositions such as "above/below" and "over/under" are given metaphoric meaning when they are applied to emotional states and feelings ("up" or "down," for instance), Savarese notes that these descriptors assume a universal, shared understanding of one's body in space, or proprioceptive reality. The way in which autistic people experience their bodies in space can differ radically from that of neurotypicals. This difference leads to alternative ways of perceiving, expressing, and describing the world. What if, Savarese asks, one does not understand the preposition "in," as in "sitting in a chair," because one experiences his body, as Mukhopadhyay does, as "scattered" in relation to the world around him (p. 279)? Proprioceptive reality, he elaborates, is "an awareness of one's body in space, an awareness of the various parts in relation to one another and their constitution as an organized and dynamic whole" (p. 283). Thinking about his voice as something he must gather and deposit into his throat, as opposed to thinking of his voice as emanating from his throat, Mukhopadhyay articulates how his sensory experiences differ from those of most others. Mukhopadhyay's understanding of his body is quite distinct from neurotypicals' proprioceptive realities and is marked by a sense that his body fuses with other bodies of matter, animate or inanimate, seamlessly. This is exemplified in his impression that his shadow is an extension of his body. Mukhopadhyay finds it difficult to sense distinct parts of his body, which feels to be at one with the world around him.

Celebrating Autistic Experiences. Savarese (2010) analyzes Mukhopadhyay's use of language in a discussion of the ways that autism can be understood as a "postcolonial neurology." He describes postcolonial neurology as "in part, a celebration of cerebral difference—in this case autism—as against the standard binaries (normal/abnormal) that customarily assign it to an inferior status," and "an acknowledgment of the history of oppression and exclusion suffered by people with autism, particularly those labeled 'severely autistic' or 'low functioning'" (p. 274). He goes on to say, "It is worth conceiving of autism in postcolonial terms because it allows us to see the current struggle for self-determination being waged by autistics as a kind of neuro-nationalist uprising and because it also frames the encounter of autistics and neurotypicals (NTs) in cosmopolitan terms" (p. 274). Rather than being defined by others (the "colonizers," who in this case are usually neurotypical "experts"), autistic people can describe their experiences, a process that can have the effect of challenging restrictive forces. In their authenticity and relevance, these descriptive expressions offer new insights into human complexity and can empower a group that historically has been oppressed.

Tapping into Creative Expression. Analyzing autistic writing provides a way to understand how autistic experience can incite new ideas about creativity. Drawing on his experiences as a creative writer and father of an autistic son, Savarese (2008, 2010) suggests that right-brain-hemispheric dominance common to nonverbal autistic people paves the way for a form of communication he terms "autie-type" (2008). Autie-type, he shares, is poetic and rich in metaphor. Savarese (2010) references a piece from *How Can I Talk If My Lips Don't Move?* in which Mukhopadhyay (2008) writes that he can "see the night jasmines wet with morning dew, lit with fresh sunshine, trying to form a story in white with their jasmine petal smell" (p. 22). Here, Mukhopadhyay gives animate license, a poetic quality, to the jasmine. In Mukhopadhyay's hands, the jasmine shows a sense of agency and is capable of formulating a story.

Combining ideas and words in unique ways, while common to many nonverbal autistic writers, is a quality that neurotypical poets strive to cultivate. Cautioning against the oversimplification of assigning discrete roles to the brain's hemispheres, Savarese (2008) notes that broadly speaking, the right hemisphere is responsible for creative endeavors and is activated in arts-based engagement. The left hemisphere, by contrast, is responsible for logic, literacy, and skills that require adherence to step-by-step processes. Savarese (2010) cites Kane (2007), who aligns the development of left-brain dominance in most humans with the shift from oral to written language use. Written language, Kane notes, solidified the shift from right-hemispheric dominance to left-hemispheric dominance in humans. Unlike many nonverbal autistic writers, in efforts to evoke fresh, creative expression, neurotypical poets must deliberately work to tune out left-hemispheric dominance in order to tap into right-hemispheric thinking. The seeming natural ability to tap into right-hemispheric associations with words, Savarese aptly observes, is a significant way that (particularly nonverbal) autistic people contribute to the enrichment and growing understanding of creative processes and expression.

An autistic person's articulation of his or her unique experiences reflects at least in part his or her verbal development and proprioceptive reality. Such articulations can have the effect of defining autism on an insider's terms. On another level, such articulations can serve political purposes, a way for a group that historically has been colonized to realize movements toward empowerment. And on yet another level, sharing one's reality serves a creative purpose, providing a way to spill one's imaginative impulses into existence. All of these effects of articulating and sharing experiences as an autistic person serve valuable purposes, both in the lives of those doing the speaking (or writing) and in the lives of those who read, respond, and interact with the ideas set forth. Importantly, a dialogue ensues, one that is far richer by the inclusion of voices that historically have been undervalued. Autistic voices, put simply, have had the qualitative effect of shifting the focus from deficit to capacity.

CREATIVE CAPACITY AS DEMONSTRATED
IN AUTISM AUTOBIOGRAPHY

A powerful creative medium that demonstrates capacities as opposed to deficits, autism autobiography has become a thriving genre. These accounts, traditionally written by people with AS who typically use speech with facility, are being fortified in larger numbers by writers who are nonverbal. While I address autism autobiography as a single genre, many writers, typically those who are nonverbal, disagree that AS and nonverbal autism belong on the same continuum (e.g., Kedar, 2012). In his autobiography *How Can I Talk If My Lips Don't Move*, Tito Mukhopadhyay (2008) reports that he does not identify with issues of social deficit that commonly are cited as central to the lives of people with AS. He shared how, desiring to connect with other kids, he thought to himself, "Perhaps . . . I could play with another boy if I got good at handling a ball" (p. 130). A disconnect between what he wished and what his body was able to perform, as opposed to an assumed disregard for other people, seems to have been a source of social isolation for Mukhopadhyay. With regard to schooling, these authors' insights are significant and can help shape understandings of relevant supports for people who have diverse abilities with respect to speech. Thus, I believe that it is useful to regard autism autobiography as a broad and diverse treasure trove of insights that can help educators and parents find ways to support autistic young people in the distinct communicative struggles they experience. In other words, both nonverbal and verbal autistic people have important contributions to make in regard to improved educational practice. Their collective work bears direct applicability to life in school and evokes ideas about how educators and schools can support creative expression and development in autistic youth.

Autism autobiography is a genre teeming with exemplars of the creative and imaginative ability of autistic people ranging in age from youth to adulthood. There is a raw quality to the younger writers' work, as they write from the trenches of navigating periods of life that are notoriously trying, especially socially—the elementary, middle, and high school years. In their work, these writers speak from the heart about the difficulties and joys of their present life, and there is a lack of the polish found in the retrospective analyses of autistic adult writers. This quality is both refreshing and effective. I chose to share these writers' work not only because they demonstrate the role that creativity and imagination have played in their sense of well-being and evolving identity, but also because of the work's recency and immediacy. Their writings resonate with other autistic youth and the families with whom those youth share their lives. Most of the young (teenage) authors featured in this chapter (with L. Jackson, 2002, and Mukhopadhyay, 2008, as exceptions) have published a book between 2011 and 2013 about life with autism. These are nonverbal autistic authors whose ability to communicate began with use of a letter board, which is a low-tech, portable board displaying the letters of the alphabet, sometimes arrayed in the manner of a traditional word-processing keyboard (QWERTY). People who use letter boards do so by pointing to letters to spell out their thoughts, word by word. Assistants can help by voicing or writing the words that form as the board user points.

Included here also for their longitudinal quality are the autobiographical writings of a few autistic adults who have produced work on a consistent basis. Their insights have culminated in a sort of collective wisdom that has been mulled, developed, and articulated over decades of life. These accounts are resplendent with numerous experiences that have taught these authors how autism, while particularly difficult in the early years, gives them an appreciated vantage point from which to engage the world. While the younger authors sometimes lament autism's difficulties and admit to at times feeling hopeless, doubtful, and despairing (see Kedar, 2012), the older writers offer a perspective of greater self-assuredness and trust of the world. This perspective is, of course, far easier to gain once one has found a life path that bears satisfaction on different fronts, including the ability to communicate with others and the ability to find work that is meaningful. The wisdom of adult autobiographers highlights elements that supported the transition from youth into adulthood and offers autistic youth, their families, and teachers ideas of how to make the transition. Several autism autobiographers have become well known in the field of autism, and they have had ample opportunity to share their ideas in public spaces such as conferences and conventions. Such is the case with Grandin, Jackson, and Mukhopadhyay, whose prolific and longstanding work I reference comprehensively in this section. Both Jackson and Mukhopadhyay represent a longitudinal navigation, of AS and autism, respectively, from childhood through early adulthood. Each wrote books in his youth (Jackson in adolescence and Mukhopadhyay at age 8) and continues to contribute to the field of autism, either through newer publications and/or presentations. Spanning a critical period of life, Jackson and Mukhopadhyay offer a unique opportunity to discern qualities that aided their successful transitions from childhood to adulthood.

Although surveying the breadth of the autism autobiography genre is beyond the scope of this book, the writers I focus on in this section demonstrate the following themes: the balance between inviting challenge and attending to natural inclinations and interests; the importance of developing interests in constructive ways; the drive for self-expression; and the need for systems of support. All of the work discussed here exemplifies the expressive capacity of autistic people, for each of the writers shows a skilled ability to engage readers with lively, colorful description, emotion, and often a witty sense of humor.

The Balance Between Inviting Challenge and Attending to Inclinations and Interests

In a discussion about his siblings, several of whom are autistic, Luke Jackson (2002) describes how his brother Ben has significant difficulty adapting to textures and sounds. Their mother, Jackson notes, works diligently to address Ben's sensitivities, and he has become slightly more comfortable touching sand and using paint, for example. Ben likewise plugs his ears often, since he finds the world generally too loud. Jackson notes the importance of his mother's work to help desensitize his brother, as he writes, "No one can spend their life with fingers in their ears" (p. 17). Along with highlighting Jackson's empathetic sense of humor, this anecdote demonstrates how he feels about identifying ways to help autistic youth reach beyond their zones of comfort and familiarity.

In a conference presentation, Jackson (2012) speaks to this topic again, emphasizing the need to branch out and expand one's repertoire of experiences, especially those that pose challenges to one's natural inclinations. However, he also highlights his realization that the most fulfilling life path takes one's propensities and natural tendencies as a guide. He shares his experiences during late adolescence trying on a variety of potential career hats. Stints as a hairdresser, a cocktail waiter, and a bookshop clerk made him keenly aware of his discomfort with an essential element of these jobs: making small talk with the people he served. While none of these jobs felt like a good fit to Jackson, his impetus to try each one reveals his need to test his limits and stretch his capacities. In *Freaks, Geeks, and Asperger Syndrome*, Jackson (2002) touches on the travails of trying to pass as "normal" versus embracing difference. He finds that he oscillates between the two, and this seems eminently clear in his willingness to put himself out there, in fields marked by the sort of light, surface-level social interaction that does not come naturally to him. Eventually, Jackson decided upon pursuing a career in photography and computer graphics, which allows him to communicate with others in ways that are more natural to him. Rather than engaging in small talk, he can delve into dialogue that is field-specific and can demonstrate his ideas through his work rather than solely through discussion.

Teenage writer Ido Kedar relatedly cites several key areas that he works on in efforts to push himself beyond his current abilities. In *Ido in Autismland*, Kedar (2012) shares that without continually practicing piano, exercising, and writing, he resorts to what he considers nonproductive, annoying habits ("stims"), such as hand-flapping. Finding that piano, exercise, and writing help channel his anxiety and sensory overload into constructive skill building, Kedar relies on these activities to maintain a sense of well-being. Writing in particular, he notes, "heals" him (p. 97), in that he is able to unload many long-harbored thoughts and ideas into material existence.

In his frustration with many aspects of autism, Kedar at times expresses a wish to be "cured" of what he refers to as a "disease" or "illness." However, traditional principles of teaching nonverbal autistic students only frustrated Kedar. His Applied Behavioral Analysis (ABA) teachers focused heavily on mastering drills and lock-step advances toward changing behaviors. His strengths, he observes, were overlooked by focusing on things he could not do. This approach lacked the flexibility and creativity that is necessary in working with students who learn in very complex ways, and Kedar similarly found traditional special education curricula watered down and dreadfully boring. Reflecting on his early childhood years, Kedar shares how as he grows older, he is learning to accept his limitations, namely, speech, bodily control, and initiating action. Instead, he believes that it is more fruitful and meaningful to focus his energy on what he can do. He notes how focusing on what he is capable of, as opposed to what is difficult for him, allows him to maintain a sense of identity that includes positive attributes. He shares, "I can't do certain things with my body no matter how much I try. I doubt I'll ever be able to sing, for example . . . I can think, point on a letter board, and type . . . if the only focus is on my speech I stay stuck because it's a disability, not an ability" (p. 93). He further notes, as quoted at the beginning of this chapter, "It's time to expand my abilities and let my disabilities live in peace" (p. 94). For Kedar, the wish to engage struggle in order to expand upon his current level of ability necessitates a concerted focus on those things he is good at doing. This is a liberating move for him, one that signifies a resistance to and a sense of freedom from the special education curricula and ABA principles that dominated his young life.

Temple Grandin likewise discusses how when she was a young girl, her mother thrust her into situations that were far from natural to her. Her mother strived to engage Grandin in the world with others, insisting that she help host cocktail parties in their home. She knew that this was a difficult undertaking for her daughter, yet held the expectation nonetheless, in an environment that integrated what was familiar (home) with an element of novelty (socializing with guests). As an adult, Grandin expresses gratitude for her mother for holding her to high expectations and for ensuring that she did not retreat from others, as she would have done left to her own devices. For Grandin (2006), intensely focusing on details, such as spinning coins or letting sand run through her fingers on the beach, was preferred over activities that required interacting with others. The attractiveness of daydreaming is understandable, as she shares, "My daydreams were like Technicolor movies in my head" (p. 101).

Grandin (2006) references another way that her mother's expectations prompted her growth in unexpected ways. Basically, her mother gave her two options during summer break: to go help on her aunt's ranch in Arizona for 2 weeks or for the whole summer. Staying home was not an option, although initially Grandin would have preferred to do so. After spending time at the ranch, however, she realized how much she enjoyed working with the animals and seeing the world from their perspectives. The ranch summers initiated Grandin's career trajectory, spurring her interest in what would become a lifelong occupation of studying animal welfare in livestock management. Here, Grandin demonstrates how accepting challenge, however uncomfortable in the beginning, led her to a career that enfolds her interests, engages her mind, and gives her opportunities to contribute meaningfully to her field, to culture, and to society.

The Importance of Developing Interests in Constructive Ways

In many ways, our culture prizes intense focus on interests. Such is the case, for instance, with medical researchers trying to isolate variables that contribute to the development of Alzheimer's disease. Or civil rights activists and humanitarians, like Martin Luther King or Mother Teresa, who made it their lifelong vocation to serve the betterment of human-ity. But when it comes to autistic youth, the topic of intense and singular focus quickly is interpreted as "obsession." Grandin (2006) asserts that because their interests in particular areas bear an even greater intensity than those of their peers, autistic youth are often ostracized. A singular focus can erode chances of enriching one's social life, for instance, since it will be more difficult to find friends who happen to share one's par-ticular interest. Cain (2012) makes a similar observation with regard to introverted youth, who often have deeper and more enduring interests, often at greater levels of sophistication, than most of their peers. These youth, she notes, need help finding like-minded others with whom they can share a social life. But for autistic youth, finding a person who shares their interests may not be as straightforward a path to building strong friendships. The high degree to which many autistic youth demonstrate their interests in a particular area may tire even the initially interested after a short while.

The rift between the social demands of young life and a greater accep-tance of intense dedication (and the solitude that often comes with it) to one's interests in adulthood commands attention. It is equally important to help autistic youth navigate the often difficult social terrain of youth as it is to support their development of interests in ways that will enrich their lives and gradually prepare them for potential vocations, careers, or hobbies that center those interests. Speaking to the latter of these con-cerns, some autistic autobiographers have noted that learning to expand one's repertoire of social skills is a useful way to find work that is mean-ingful. Other times, autistic writers notice how accepting one's social style leads to a truly satisfying life. Jackson (2012) discusses how he initially thought that a savvier ability to integrate socially might offer him oppor-tunities to find a meaningful career path in life. However, upon trying out a diverse array of jobs that required him to make small talk with clients, he found himself stressed and anxious. For Jackson, the realization that a career in the computer and art worlds better suited his personality led him to a sense of self-acceptance. He no longer feels the need to apologize for who he is, nor does he feel the pressure to engage with the social ease that most neurotypicals do.

Although they represent different approaches to finding a path that led them to fulfilling careers, both Grandin and Jackson suggest that finding ways to work with difficult aspects of autism is key to finding a satisfying life trajectory. Trial and error also can enhance one's sense of self-acceptance, which is a critical piece of finding meaningful life work. Grandin finds it incredibly important for autistic students to integrate hands-on work into their curricular goals. She expresses deep concern (2006, 2013) for autistic youth and what she observes to be their growing interest in video games. In a 2013 talk at the Chicago Humanities Festival, she called for a stronger arts-based agenda in schools and for classes such as cooking, metal shop, woodworking, and sewing. Grandin credits her very early penchant for drawing and painting, and the enthusiastic encouragement in these areas she received from others, as the foundation for her ability to succeed as a scientist. She shares that she was invited and encouraged to do all kinds of art in school and that without art she would have been "nowhere."

These reflections suggest the very critical responsibility of educators and parents to help steer autistic youth in constructive ways with their interests as guides. Grandin laments the propensity for contemporary youth to engage in activities that do not help them develop fine and gross motor skills. It is in the process of creating something with one's hands, she notes, that the development of resourcefulness, a quality of creative thinking, takes place. When one encounters frustration on a given project (say, woodworking), and things do not go as planned or as visualized, one is put in the position to rework a new plan for construction. In this process, one must consider and work within the confines of restraint, with what materials are available, with the skill set one has, and so on. This process, significantly, integrates the mind and the body. She (2013) firmly believes that autistic youth must "learn how to do work" and that it is adults' job "to get them out . . . doing things." Her (2006) concern is centered on the reality that many autistic youth who are able to successfully complete academic programs are underemployed. Attention to problem-solving activities common to the arts and trades, and a re-emphasis on these types of activities in schools, offers a way for autistic youth to develop skills necessary to feel ready for and competent in a number of fields.

Both Grandin and Jackson express concern about autistic youths' transition into adulthood. Jackson (2012) asserts the critical importance of encouraging the interests of these youth early and earnestly. He believes that schools need to have organized structures in place to support autistic kids, all along the way. Like Grandin, he mentions human supports such as friends, tutors, and so on. Grandin (2013) seems to feel that differentiation, such as letting students do more challenging math if they can do it, even when it means diverging from the planned curricula, and inclusion of hands-on skills are important. Together, these qualities can keep students engaged in school and help them develop skills to prepare them for jobs in the world beyond the structure of academic learning. Here, Grandin takes both the long and the short views: She attends to what is immediately necessary (staying engaged in school), as well as what is necessary for students' longstanding goals, dreams, and career promise. Both Grandin and Jackson agree that channeling obsessions and deep interests into things that other people value can help autistic youth develop their interests into viable skills. In the development of interests into viable skills, a path to authentic integration can be paved, where autistic people can do work that they enjoy while making valuable social and cultural contributions.

A Drive to Express Oneself

Although Jackson tried jobs in a number of industries before deciding to pursue a career in photography and graphic art, his interest in creative pursuits was constant. At a 2012 conference, Jackson and his mother attested that since the age of 5, Jackson played around with photography in some capacity. Along with the autobiographical work he produced at an early age, Jackson published a book of poetry in 2006, *Crystalline Lifetime: Fragments of Asperger Syndrome*. Interestingly, despite his prolific writing career, when he discusses interests, Jackson does not mention writing. Rather, he cites computers as a lifelong passion, one that, as a teenager, he had hoped to pursue into adulthood with a career in programming. Jackson's attention to aesthetic qualities of computers can be interpreted as a foreshadowing of his eventual career choice in graphic art. In 2002, he wrote, "I often daydream about what backdrop I could have and what colour scheme I could use for my taskbar and message boxes" (p. 45). As a writer, a photographer, and a graphic artist, Jackson has engaged in creative processes all his life. And while he doesn't directly state the need to engage in creativity in his younger years, Jackson's actions reveal this reality. His work often has bridged his imaginative abilities with practical use, as he has used creative forms to connect with others and to share his written work as a resource for those with AS.

Neither Elizabeth Bonker nor Naoki Higashida (2013) speaks, although both teenagers convey their thoughts and ideas imaginatively through words. In the book *I Am in Here* (Bonker & Breen, 2011), Bonker writes poetry and then translates her poems into terse paragraphs that explain the meanings of her poems. Bonker's poetry is spiritual and explores identity and self-acceptance. In a poem titled "Bright Future," for instance, she writes, "When you see a tree, think of me growing strong and tall . . . When you see the water on the lake think of the future I plan to make . . . Me strong mighty free" (p. 15). The sense of optimism in Bonker's poem, however, belies her thoughts about certain experiences. According to Virginia Breen, Bonker's mother and coauthor, one of the first words she expressed when learning to use a letter board was "agony." When her teacher, Soma Mukhopadhyay (mother of Tito), asked if she knew what agony meant, Bonker replied, "Quite so" (Breen & Bonker, 2012). The girl went on to type about the frustration she felt wanting to talk but not being able to do so. Bonker's yearning to connect with other people through conversation has prompted Breen to question the continuing use of the term "autism," which translates as "self-centered." She calls instead for a conceptualization that reflects updated knowledge about autism, noting how despite not speaking, her daughter does in fact hear, think, learn, and desire to communicate with others.

Similarly, David Mitchell (2013), who wrote the introduction to Higashida's *The Reason I Jump*, asserts, "Emotional poverty and an aversion to company are not *symptoms* of autism but *consequences* of autism, its harsh lockdown on self-expression and society's near-pristine ignorance about what's happening inside autistic heads" (p. xv, emphasis in original). Recall too that the idea of dispelling the myth of autism as a person alone also was engaged by Biklen (2005) and his coauthors. Creative forms of communication, such as poetry and storytelling, are often the preferred genres that nonspeaking autistic people use to communicate their experiences. It is no overstatement to say that the ability to discern the thoughts of nonspeaking autistic people is leading to a monumental change in the way that autism is understood. As methods of communication make it possible for nonspeaking autistic people to share their ideas, our culture is enriched by the descriptions, often creative, of what life can be like for a population that historically has been outcast and misunderstood.

Higashida (2013) writes in a direct, question-and-answer format, and much of his writing evidences an acute sense of perception, a sensitivity to beauty, and a vivid inner life. In response to the question, "Why are your facial expressions so limited?" he writes, "What makes us smile from the inside is seeing something beautiful, or a memory that makes us laugh" (p. 31). To the question, "What causes panic attacks and meltdowns?" Higashida asserts, "One of the biggest misunderstandings you have about us is your belief that our feelings aren't as subtle and complex as yours" (p. 109). He clearly demonstrates the ability to imagine others' perceptions and to engage in direct dialogue.

Yet Higashida, who had hoped since childhood to become the writer he has become, dedicates the last chapter of his book to a piece of creative writing titled, "I'm Right Here." There, he explores spiritual themes such as life after death, reincarnation, and figuring out how to cope with loss. The main character of the story is Shun, a boy who has just died. The story follows the trajectory of Shun as he realizes that he has died, as he tries in vain to comfort his devastated parents, as he tries to decide between living in heaven forever or being reincarnated as a new baby born to his parents, and so on. The story references Higashida's life in metaphorical ways. He says that he wrote the story to give readers a sense of what it is like to yearn to express oneself to a loved one without being able to do so effectively. In the story, there are many scenes where Shun tries to talk to his parents, to apologize for leaving them, and to help comfort them in the wake of his death. They never can hear him, and, as a result, Shun cannot rest peacefully. In one scene, Shun comes to grips with what reincarnation would mean to him, to his unique sense of identity. He thinks to himself, "So there won't be any Me anymore. . . . My existence will be wiped out forever. . . . Now Shun understood a bit better why Kazuo and his other friends were staying on so long in Heaven" (p. 128). In the end, Shun observes his mother close to death in a hospital, sick with heartbreak for having lost Shun. At that moment, Shun chooses to save his mother's life by relinquishing his identity and his memories in favor of reincarnating as a baby girl that his parents name Nozomi. In this way, Shun lives on and reinvigorates his parents' spirits and their will to live. His parents' misery is transformed into joy and contentedness. It is a story replete with imaginative dialogue, vibrant imagery, and a main character who demonstrates an earnest sense of searching.

Expressiveness also comes in the form of sharing one's experiences to pave a smoother path for others. A sentiment that both Kedar and Mukhopadhyay share is that while they still experience ongoing struggles related to autism, their ability to communicate with clarity in writing affords them a unique opportunity. Mukhopadhyay (2008) speaks to the power of education (he credits his mother Soma as his best and constant teacher) as a catalyst for his expressive abilities: "It was education that helped me enrich my imagination with all those probable and improbable reasonings based on science and philosophy, so that I could write my imaginings down as stories or as poetry" (p. 214). Neither Mukhopadhyay nor Kedar expresses certainty about what his future holds in personal or professional terms, yet each finds significance in the possibility that the contributions he has made in writing books have been beneficial to other nonverbal autistic people and their supporters. Mukhopadhyay asserts,

> With my physical and neurological limitations, I am unable to do certain kinds of work. But I can think. And I can write. I can write down my stories on paper with my pencil. Perhaps all those stories, written and waiting to be written, will be my contribution to society. (p. 216)

Writing can be as personally constructive as it can be a social contribution. Kedar (2012) observes, "It's good to know I need to write about my feelings to have more self-autonomy and self-awareness . . . I need to write to stay focused in reality. . . . If not, I swirl internally in my inner life" (p. 97). He further asserts, "I will continue to write my journey for myself because now I see that writing heals me" (p. 97). In that these authors have employed their hard-earned communication skills to tell about their lives with autism, they have contributed generously to a culture that continues to grapple with autism's meanings.

The Need for Systems of Support

Kedar (2012) experienced more than 10 years of behavioral interventions aimed at helping to "normalize" him. ABA specialists carried out rote, lock-step lessons; wore blank expressions; and rewarded him with food and tickles for answering correctly. Kedar, unsurprisingly, felt patronized by these "rewards," and his progress was incremental at best. His mother, Tracy Kedar, who writes the introductory section of her son's book, explains that doubt regarding ABA did not set in until she told his teachers about the communicative strides he had made at home. There, he was able to do some writing and could respond with relevance to questions his parents asked him. The ABA team expressed their disbelief and said that these strides were not possible for Kedar, who they had determined to be mentally retarded. This system of support, however well intended it may have been, assumed very little of Kedar, and in the end the rigidity of the approach and of the ABA team forced the family to other means of support for their son. Through a reference, they found Soma Mukhopadhyay, mother of Tito, who worked with Kedar, teaching him to communicate his thoughts with clarity using a letter board. Through her teaching, Soma demonstrated a belief in Kedar's competence and intelligence. She engaged him wholly, using rapid speech, quick motion, and multiple modalities simultaneously (e.g., writing out words while saying them as she wrote, and then ripping the words from the paper to present to him). She held him to high expectations and did not offer rewards, but instead gave him grade-appropriate learning goals and curricula. Although there was a difficult adjustment period during which Kedar resisted Soma's high expectations, he responded well to her style of teaching and, significantly, to her clear, immediate belief in his abilities. For teaching him a way to communicate that allows him to express his ideas as he wishes, Kedar (2012) credits her for having helped him build a communication "raft" (p. 97) and for having "saved his life" (p. 35).

In his book, a compilation of journal entries between the ages of 12 and 15, Kedar (2012) shares the deep frustrations he encountered growing up autistic. The pain he felt as a very young child was rooted in his inability to communicate his thoughts, and the social ramifications of this inability. Throughout the book, Kedar makes a plea for generalizing the use of letter boards in teaching nonverbal autistic youth to communicate. Withholding the tool, he thinks, is a form of cruelty. He notes, "To deny communication is a crime against humanity. It is cruel in result if not intention" (p. 56). Although he does not claim the letter board to be a panacea for all that he finds difficult about being autistic, learning to use it has given him a concrete tool with which to engage conversationally in the world. It has freed him to share his thoughts and his ideas, and generally demonstrate that he is an intelligent person, despite what his behaviors might suggest. Importantly, the use of the letter board allowed Kedar to finally feel like himself. "I'm telling you," he shares, "it was like being born into me" (p. 59).

Grandin (2006) believes that everyday interactions in routines such as dinnertime, games with neighborhood kids, and small talk with houseguests helped her acquire basic skills that paved the way for her to enter a profession that has posed many obstacles to her. Her field, for one, traditionally was populated with men, as very few women worked in livestock management. Her entry into the field was likewise difficult because of her awkward habits, intonation, and unique way of dressing. The quality that she refers to as one of the most helpful through these difficult roadblocks was knowing that she needed mentors. Locating human-support systems such as unconventional, nonjudgmental teachers, managers in the field, and friends within the community helped Grandin navigate many murky waters. Such was the case when she began college and was struggling in French and in math. With the help of a teacher, Mr. Carlock, who agreed to tutor her in these subjects every week, Grandin passed the classes. She likewise cites a governess who cared for her during childhood as a person whose early influence helped her become aware of safety rules and general social graces. Several field-specific mentors, in her adult years, have provided needed guidance in navigating social situations that were ambiguous or that contributed to tensions among Grandin and her colleagues.

THE ALIGNMENT IN SUM

In contemporary scholarship, creativity is broadly understood to be the act of contributing novel ideas, interpretations, or solutions to issues or problems that bear relevance to one's reality (Beghetto & Kaufman, 2013). Pursuing one's personal potential is another manifestation of creativity, as it is understood in modernity (Ogata, 2013). There seems to be agreement that creative work generally serves some purpose, respects certain parameters, and, at its best, bears meaning to those who engage the work (Amabile, 1997). All of this is to say that creative work does not entail pulling ideas out of thin air, solely "thinking outside of the box," or abandoning one's knowledge base and reality for the sake of sheer originality. In the words of creativity researchers Beghetto and Kaufman (2010), contrary to common belief, creativity is not characterized by "unconstrained originality" (p. 193). Contemporary understandings of creativity hold that creative work builds a proverbial bridge between the established and the possible, meshing what is known with what is yet unrealized in the construction of something new. Vygotsky (1967/2004) shared this notion, attesting that "imagination always builds using materials supplied by reality" (p. 14). One's imagination—a conglomeration of cultural influences, traditions, prior knowledge, and visions for the future—ignites a creative impulse. Through a process of creativity, an individual thought or endeavor can invoke collaboration: One might fuse an original thought or endeavor with the ideas of others, including those that constitute one's prior knowledge. Likewise, what begins as an individual impulse may evolve into a contribution that can be witnessed, evaluated, enjoyed, and critiqued by the social world. Creative processes entail both individual and collaborative engagement.

The diverse renderings of autistic expression in this chapter demonstrate features of creativity, as it is discussed in contemporary scholarship, in a multitude of ways. There are manners of thinking that convey thoughtful introspection and innovative problem solving, as is the case, for instance, with Osler, Frugone, and Blackman. With Emily, there is playfulness, despite limited speech, that evidences a distinct wish to connect and build human relationships. Hay and Winn (2005) highlight the spontaneous instinct for self-preservation displayed by the boy who stood up to a bully with reciprocal force. There are likewise exemplars of humor, wit, and creative writing that are intricately tied to authors' experiences with autism, as demonstrated in autism autobiography. In their insights, some of those featured in this chapter demonstrate how anger can drive one to work toward constructive change. Such is the case with Osler's letter writing to his school professionals as well as Grandin's outrage at a lack of arts-based, tactile learning experiences for autistic youth. Some also express frustration and exhaustion with the current state of affairs regarding communicative tools. These strong emotions likewise propel the impulse to promote change. Kedar emphasized throughout his book that his focus on communicative opportunities for nonverbal autistic youth was tied to his own experiences and spurred his goal to pursue a career in autism and education. This sentiment comes as no surprise, given his unwavering vision for a more equitable future for others who share his struggles with nonverbal autism. Likewise, Bonker's palpable knowledge of the meaning of "agony" speaks volumes about her wish for communication to be more readily available to nonverbal autistic people. Her clear ability to think, perceive, and process the world beckons a reevaluation of the term "autism" to describe a way of being that is very much connected to the lives of others.

Within the collective insights demonstrated in this chapter, there are also quiet celebrations for hard-earned self-acceptance, often after years of difficulty and coming to terms with the hardships that autism can bring. Grandin, Jackson, Kedar, Higashida, and Mukhopadhyay each discuss significant gifts that come with autism as well, such as focus, perceptiveness, empathy, and the ability to share one's insights in hopes of facilitating smoother experiences for other autistic youth. The people featured in this chapter have made social contributions and are part of a broad cultural change under way. Their ability to think and write or otherwise communicate their ideas is a collective force that imparts to the field a degree of richness it has never seen before.

CHAPTER 3

Autism, Creativity, and the Arts

For me, being labeled on the spectrum while having my sense of creativity is like a double-edged sword. Sometimes it can be dangerous, but at times it is a great advantage for me.

—Vincent Mazzone

In this chapter, I focus on the work and insights of several autistic artists. As a group, they articulate key skills, abilities, and qualities that the arts bring to their lives. In many ways, it appears that the benefits of creative engagement are no different for autistic people than for anybody else. Those featured in this chapter, however, demonstrate how qualities elemental to or cultivated by being autistic actually can play a supporting role in their ability to engage creatively. They likewise illuminate how creativity can temper many of the struggles that they encounter. Significantly, these contributors attest that autism offers a distinct vantage point from which to understand and engage creativity. As discussed in Chapter 2, Savarese (2010) notes how one's physical relationship with the world directly impacts his or her interpretations of life events. Linneman's (2001) description of Emily offers an example of how corporeal circumstances influence responses to events of everyday living. In her computer work, Emily used nonverbal expressive means to communicate and build a relationship with Linneman.

It is likewise the case that qualities reportedly shared by many autistic people, such as a desire for structure and a deep sense of commitment to one's own interests, have the potential to provide advantageous opportunities for creative expression. Further, the artists illuminate how the cultural environments in which they live exert as much influence on their responses to the world as does their neurological or physical constitution. This influence includes attitudinal atmosphere, or how their ways of being are interpreted and judged by others. Artistic expression gives autistic people the chance to process and respond to others' interpretations of their ways of being. In this way, art helps each individual develop his or her personal voice and perspective, and contribute to an ongoing dialogue about what autism means.

In the first section of this chapter, I introduce a nuanced system of creativity that can be useful to classroom teachers. Drawing on this creativity scholarship, I highlight the ways that qualities of creativity and autism can build on and support one another. As the autistic artists featured in this chapter demonstrate, their quality of life is enriched in the engagement of arts-based creativity. The arts, they attest, are a forum for emotional expression, prompt the engagement of struggle and movement beyond comfort zones, develop and demonstrate perspective and voice, and provide a channel for propensities and enduring interests.

A FINER GRAINED CONCEPTION OF CREATIVITY

As discussed in Chapter 2, there has been only a slight shift within autism scholarship from a focus on Big-C contributions to little-c forms. In this chapter, I continue to address this needed shift. The chapter enfolds the perspectives of autistic people in discussing, demonstrating, and otherwise representing creativity in diverse artistic forms. Two of the contributors included later in the chapter, Tito Mukhopadhyay and Larry Bissonnette, engage a level of creativity that aligns with a professional, or "Pro-C" level of creativity. Pro-C is a form of creativity described in a four-tiered, developmental system articulated by creativity scholars Beghetto and Kaufman (2013). Offering a finer grained interpretation of creativity than the broad little-c/Big-C construct, their scheme ranks mini-c, little-c, Pro-C, and Big-C forms of creativity. This tiered system is particularly useful for classroom teachers working with students who demonstrate varying levels of creative development. Mini-c is a creative form that is termed "interpretive," and this level is readily observed when a student discovers a new approach to solving a problem. An example might be when a student replaces a method for solving math problems with a more sophisticated approach. He or she may move from using a concrete method that includes the use of object manipulatives to using mental math to solve problems with greater fluidity and automaticity. Little-c creativity is related, although more complex, and the authors give the following scenario as an example: "a 10th grade social studies class developing an original project that combines learning about a key historical event with gathering local histories from community elders" (p. 12). Another example of little-c creativity might be a 5th-grade social studies project that calls for creating recipes for a week's worth of family meals based on ingredients locally available to 17th-century settlers in a specific region of the Atlantic Coast. (This project also could be thematic, integrating math, nutritional or environmental science, literacy, and culinary art, for example.)

By contrast, Pro-C is an "expert" level of creativity represented by those who contribute innovations that are significant yet not legendary.

Beghetto and Kaufman (2013) highlight discrete and field-enhancing contributions, such as the flipped classroom "pioneered by teachers Aaron Sams and Jonathan Bergmann" (p. 12), as exemplary Pro-C contributions. The final tier, Big-C, contains "legendary" contributions such as the revolutionary approach to early childhood education developed by Maria Montessori (p. 13). Her approach continues to have wide reach and influence in school programs globally. The previous chapter highlighted several Pro-C contributors, notably those who have published autism autobiography. An exception is Grandin, who can be understood as a Big-C contributor in part by virtue of having been the first person to provide an insider's perspective on autism. In that she was a pioneer in changing the way people think about autism, and because her ideas have had a remarkably wide reach, her contributions are arguably legendary.

For Beghetto and Kaufman (2013), it is critical to highlight how each of these levels might be engaged in classrooms and schools. While the first two levels are directly relevant in this regard, they note that the latter two levels can be integrated into curricula by introducing significant individuals, for instance, those who have performed at these levels of creativity. One example might be to invite parents or community members (e.g., authors, scientists, or artists who make a living with their craft) into the classroom to give presentations about their Pro-C contributions or to share experiences on the job. Likewise, Big-C contributors can be referenced in various units of study. For example, educators can weave biographies and autobiographies of notable leaders and innovators into curricula and make them available for student use. In articulating a wide-reaching view of creativity, Beghetto and Kaufman contribute an interpretation of creativity that is inclusive. Their tiered structure has a place for everyone, and any interest, to learn and evolve beyond current capacities.

AUTISTIC ARTISTS AND WHY THEY ENGAGE WITH THE ARTS

For several years, I have followed the work of artists and autism self-advocates Tito Mukhopadhyay and Larry Bissonnette, becoming familiar with them through their scholarly publications and other media. In this book, they prove to be rich resources for broadening understandings of the relationship between autism and creativity. Both Bissonnette and Mukhopadhyay, through painting and poetry writing, respectively, have amassed a range of work that has been published and displayed in various venues. Three other artists are featured in this chapter as well and discussed in greater detail later. Vincent Mazzone, Sarah Gaines, and Henry Goldsmith are young adults whose illustrations, musicality, and performance were among the creative works that contributed to the inspiration for writing this book.

Although I have integrated the insights and ideas of Mukhopad-hyay in Chapter 2, here I focus exclusively on the poetic quality that is portrayed in his linguistic expression. Now living in Texas, Mukhopad-hyay is from Bangalore, India, and is in his mid-20s. He has published his written work, both poetry and autobiography, for over a decade. His writing frequently explores life with nonverbal autism, and his perceptions have added depth and complexity to a growing understanding of what autism means. The accessibility of his work, as well as his willingness to share his time and thoughts with others, makes Mukho-padhyay a strong contributor to any competence-based discussion of autism. During the summer of 2013, Mukhopadhyay and I shared emails regarding the nature of his poetry and his perspective on the way his proprioceptive reality (or awareness of his body in space) influences his work. In the fall of 2014, we again shared emails regarding creativity and schooling. I reference these strands of discussion as supplemental to the poetry I include in this chapter.

Bissonnette is a prolific painter working and living in Vermont. Now in his 50s, he has been creating artwork since childhood and works from a studio that houses a copious supply of paintings he has made over time. He types to communicate, and as his participation in the documentary film *Wretches and Jabberers* (Wurzburg, 2011) attests, Bissonnette is as commandingly expressive with his typed words as with his actions. His contributions through writing, painting, and film have exposed his wit, dedication, and sense of deep connectedness to others. In early 2011, I attended a (*New York*) *Times Talk* where Bissonnette, in the company of fellow advocate Tracy Thresher, shared his experiences making *Wretches and Jabberers*. Bissonnette, who typed, engaged the audience with humor, honesty, and frankness about his commitment to forwarding the conception of autism as difference as opposed to deficit. His sentiments at the *Times Talk* echoed those he shared in *Wretches and Jabberers*, which at times offer context to his creative process and artwork. For this reason, and because his participation in the film evidences a different form of creative engagement, I reference the film in this chapter along with his paintings.

Like these men, the other three contributors in this chapter spend time regularly engaged in creative work. Yet at this juncture in their lives, none engages his or her creativity on a professional level. In contrast to Mukhopadhyay and Bissonnette, Henry Goldsmith, Vincent Mazzone, and Sarah Gaines use speech with facility. I have known each of them since 2003. Goldsmith and Mazzone were my students for 2 consecutive years when I was an elementary classroom teacher. Although I was never Gaines's teacher, I met her when she was beginning middle school, through her mother, who was a teaching colleague.

Goldsmith is now 21 years old and recently finished his second semester at Berklee College of Music in Boston. A musician who has been playing guitar since elementary school, Goldsmith was in a band through-out middle and high school, and there are traces of this stage of his life to be found on YouTube videos (2010a, 2010b). He likewise composes and records music, hopes to tour with a rock/heavy metal band, and states that an ultimate goal is to "see more of the world, to become less xeno-phobic and better myself as a man" (H. Goldsmith, personal communica-tion, March 13, 2013).

At 22, Mazzone recently finished his fourth year of college at the School of Visual Arts (SVA) in New York City. He studies cartoon illus-tration, notes that his favorite avenue of creativity is "drawing wacky cartoon characters," and has a longstanding goal to "show my creations to the world, and be the next big hit in the cartooning business" (V. Maz-zone, personal communication, March 13, 2013). Mazzone has been making illustrations for years, and I recall that, during my years teaching him, drawing was the activity he would turn to first upon completing any assigned work. Drawing was what he always chose to do when he had free time.

Gaines, 25, graduated from college with a degree in psychology, a minor in Spanish, and an enduring interest in acting and theater perfor-mance. She had opportunities to explore her creative medium in a public high school dedicated to developing students' talents in performing arts. Some of Gaines's performance art is captured in YouTube videos she has made. Like Goldsmith, Gaines (2013) demonstrates how YouTube is a valuable and accessible resource for archiving one's creative endeavors and tracking one's creative development. These days, Gaines is also a pro-lific knitter and crocheter, and these activities have been significant cre-ative outlets for her as well.

Through the sharing of thoughts and ideas around creativity by way of email discussions among the four of us beginning in the winter of 2013 (with follow-ups through the fall of 2014), Gaines, Mazzone, and Gold-smith articulated the vital role that creativity has played in their lives. Our conversations brought to the fore the abilities and skills that are de-veloped as a result of dedicating oneself to a chosen art form. All three of these contributors are natives of New York City, and all have been actively engaged in artistic forms of creativity for many years. Through their vari-ous arts-based interests, each has cultivated an identity for him- or her-self that is inclusive of a multitude of strengths, and these strengths have supported their ability to tackle difficult aspects of daily life, within and beyond the parameters of school.

Collectively, the voices and demonstrations of the artists represented in this chapter underscore how their creative expression cannot be di-vorced from autism. That is, they represent autism to be not merely a part of who they are, but as constituting a way of being with qualities that infiltrate everything they do, creatively and otherwise. The artists under-score several ways that the arts cultivate an enriched quality of life. The arts, they demonstrate, afford them emotional expression, give them the opportunity to engage struggle and move beyond comfort zones, provide a forum for developing and expressing personal voice and perspective, and provide a channel for propensities and enduring interests.

Affording Emotional Expression

Arts-based activities engage one's emotions in a number of ways. The artists share how emotions can evoke creative expression and how participation in their chosen form of art can help mitigate, manage, understand, or process difficult emotions. At other times, they demonstrate how creative work allows them to express emotions of gratitude. They further show how benefits of participating in their chosen art form include increased energy and commitment to their art and a sense of connectedness to others.

Increased Energy. The role that music has played in Goldsmith's life, for example, has been significant to developing his communicative abilities. "Therapeutically," he explains, "music has helped me break through my autistic shell. When I was young, language was beyond my grasp and it frustrated me. Music was a way for me to vent and express myself" (H. Goldsmith, personal communication, March 21, 2013). He goes on to discuss his process of writing music, illuminating the role that emotions play in that process. He shares,

> Creativity is like a spark. It is a burning feeling that comes from my emotions at any given time that needs to be released. For me it happens musically and in verse. Often when I feel good, I play random bits of ideas, chords, progression, and runs of major, minor, pentatonic or chromatic scales and arpeggios on my guitar. When depressed or frustrated, that sparks me to write short poems on scrap paper to capture that moment while that creative "spark" is bright. (H. Goldsmith, personal communication, March 21, 2013)

The expressive release that Goldsmith refers to is evident in his YouTube videos. These videos, which feature his School of Rock (SOR) band performing with well-known guest musicians Dee Snider and Joe Lynn Turner, are visual demonstrations of Goldsmith's great excitement at the opportunity to play with these legends. Performing the Twisted Sister song "We're Not Gonna Take It" with Dee Snider, Goldsmith pumps his fists in the air and bobs his head in a rhythm reminiscent of glam rockers of the 1980s. Onstage, he plays guitar behind his back, freely reels his arms, cups his hand over his ear to prompt audience response, and shares the microphone with Snider (Goldsmith, 2010b). Similarly, when his SOR band played with another idol, rock musician Joe Lynn Turner,

Goldsmith posted the following caption on his YouTube video recording of the performance: "one of the BEST NIGHT [sic] OF MY LIFE! I Got to Play With JOE LYNN TURNER on ALL RIGHT NOW! Not the best quality, but its AWSM!!!" (Goldsmith, 2010a).

Goldsmith regards these moments as highlights in his life as a musician, although equally important to his memories is the approachability of these musical legends. Discussing meeting Snider, he explains,

> I met Dee Snider prior to performing with him at a School of Rock "Best of Season" show where I did Stevie Ray Vaughn's rendition of "Texas Flood". After leaving the stage, Dee shook my hand and said I was great. It was one of the best moments of playing live. A few years later, I was performing with Dee on his rock anthem "We're Not Gonna Take It." I remember backstage before the performance that Dee was SOO nice to all of us All Stars. He was taking pictures with all of the students and the kids, and he took the time to let me talk to him about Heavy Metal music. It was stupefyingly AWESOME. I always remember Dee as a great performer, but mostly as a great person. (H. Goldsmith, personal communication, June 13, 2013)

At a basic level, music offers Goldsmith a vehicle for emotional expression. Difficult emotions such as depression or frustration can be transformed, in the process of making music, to excitement, joy, and contentedness. But on another level, life as a musician also gives Goldsmith opportunities to connect with others, such as those in his band as well as mentors. Band participation provided him with the opportunity to learn from professionals about better musicianship, including the importance of reaching out to aspiring musicians and being an encouraging role model. A creative force that seems to give back as much as it requires of his energy, music is a way of life for Goldsmith and a context for building numerous relevant skills and abilities.

Stress Reduction. Mazzone similarly discusses how he often employs his work as an illustrator to help him deal with strong emotions. Of a free draw that he calls "The Anime Version of Dante's Inferno" (see Figure 3.1), Mazzone explains, "The Inferno represents going through pure HELL and facing your demons to get to your loved ones" (personal communication, June 7, 2013). In fleshing out this sentiment, Mazzone exposes how difficult aspects of life are mitigated by a focus on getting a specific task done and finding support in significant others along the way. He explains, "There will be tough days when you feel so much pressure from completing a final draft. . . . However, if you focus on the task given to you and do it very well, then you will be able to overcome your own doubts and get the credit you deserve" (V. Mazzone, personal communication, June 25,

Figure 3.1. Dante's Inferno

2013). Noting that much of the difficulty that he encounters is spurred by a sense of feeling overwhelmed, anxiety, and self-doubt, Mazzone factors the unconditional support of his loved ones into his ability to manage tough days and difficult projects. He feels that "no matter how hard you work, being with your family and friends is the best way to get through hardship and struggles" (V. Mazzone, personal communication, June 25, 2013).

Connectedness to Others. Mazzone's reference to his family as a pivotal system of support highlights the role of human connection in the process of creative work. As an activist and a painter, Bissonnette also expresses a deep appreciation for the people throughout his life who have provided him with support and companionship.

At times difficult to follow, Bissonnette's metaphoric use of language conveys complex ideas. Biklen (2005) observes how Bissonnette's writing "is rich in visual images and often leaves me trying to unpack it, as if reading poetry, to understand his points . . . Larry's images and vocabulary are captivating" (p. 169). Bissonnette's linguistic expression in the film *Wretches and Jabberers* (Wurzburg, 2011) reveals his regard for other people. During the film, Bissonnette's travel partner and fellow autistic self-advocate, Tracy Thresher, asks Bissonnette about whether he thought eating sushi was a highlight of their trip to Japan. In response, Bissonnette emphasizes his enjoyment of the people over the food, sharing, "Plenty of lovely people makes me look at going places like Japan as building new lines of communication between people of meaningfully lasting temperaments so more about people than food." In finding like-minded individuals the world over, Bissonnette expands his circle of allies and aligns with others who exhibit what he calls a "penchant for language as a loud spear for bursting bubbles of backwards thinking about people who don't get to speak normally." Bissonnette highlights how the quality of community, forged through a shared love of language and an inability to speak with fluency, makes his work meaningful and worthwhile.

As is the case with his typing, Bissonnette's appreciation for people comes through with clarity in his artwork. For each of the 16 paintings featured in the chapter he shared with Biklen (Bissonnette, 2005), he includes commentary description. His comments for the piece titled "Very pale Ray, temporary roommate" reflect on his years spent in an institution for people with developmental disabilities: "My pent-up time in tested for learning patterns of best behavior institution wasn't entirely greys; it offered personal periods of great relationships with friends with disabilities" (p. 175). The painting is a long, rectangular canvas bordered by raw wood framing. Its palette consists of white, blues, and brownish reds, and the latter shade is primarily represented in what might be a tree branch that spans the horizon of the canvas. There is additionally a Polaroid photograph layered upon part of the branch, a portrait of a person who appears to be smiling. For another piece titled "Seeing Eye Friend Felicia in gathering of my very canned together speech," he provides the following commentary: "Larry's somewhat bastardization of English language puts friends in the role of interpreters extraordinaire" (p. 175). This piece, a bold composition of a blue sky and a large deeply red house with several windows and a door or two, likewise features a Polaroid photograph of a person who smiles for the camera.

Bissonnette's dedication to and descriptions of the friends he made while living in the institution reveal moments of buoyancy and trust offsetting apparently insipid living conditions. As the centering of others in his paintings suggests, friends play several important roles in his life. They are crucial antidotes to "grey" periods of life, provide him with company and camaraderie, and act as allies in his promotion of constructive understandings of autism. A scene in *Wretches and Jabberers* elucidates the gratitude and joy with which Bissonnette regards his friendships. When Thresher notes, "I think that this has been the trip of a lifetime, Larry, and

I'm so happy that we did it together," Bissonnette replies, "Larry loops you twice on that loving trip fellowship feeling."

Engaging Struggle and Movement Beyond Comfort Zones

While autism clearly entails struggle, not every autistic person interprets challenge and struggle in the same way. Mazzone and Gaines, for instance, approach struggle quite differently. While Mazzone laments the continual challenge that feelings of frustration represent in his life, Gaines is driven toward challenge. She actively seeks experiences that will stretch her capacities as a person and as an artist. Although these two express different ways of regarding struggle, each nonetheless engages and grows from struggle, and in his and her own way has located systems of support to help work through struggle in efforts to move beyond current abilities.

Development of Strategies. Mazzone's articulation of autism illuminates a sense of tension that can threaten his ability to create. "When I think of the word 'autistic' or 'autism' or 'Asperger syndrome,'" Mazzone shares, "I think about two thoughts itching at the back of my skull at the exact same time." He elaborates,

> It is nerve-wracking at times, but I still manage to figure everything out by taking the ideas one step at a time. For me, being labeled on the spectrum while having my sense of creativity is like a double-edged sword. Sometimes it can be dangerous, but at times it is a great advantage for me. (V. Mazzone, personal communication, March 15, 2013)

He later appends, "If I get too creative on a small project it backfires on my original plans on making it, and vice versa" (V. Mazzone, personal communication, March 19, 2013). Giving too much of his creative energy to a small-scale project can sting him as readily as giving too little creative energy to larger scale projects. Working on ways to allocate one's creative energy and resources is a point of Mazzone's learning curve with which he struggles. Art school gives him the support, space, and structure in which to develop field-relevant skills, and he likewise relies on an extensive support system outside of school to help him meet demanding tasks.

Mazzone's struggles with frustration are a part of life that he has become used to, and he is strengthened by routine and the knowledge of what others' expectations are for him. External supports and prompts from others are critical to his ability to find his way through situations that he deems uncomfortable. He explains,

> I do sometimes feel frustrated [when] out of my comfort zone, but moreover the frustration comes to me by my own self-doubts. For

example, "This is too hard, I can't do it," or "I'll never be good enough to accomplish this task, etc." However, I have managed to control my anger and my self-doubts most of the time, and I do have help from my family, friends, and Group [of other autistic people]. . . . As long as they believe I can go the distance, I believe in myself a lot more and overcome any obstacles in my way. (V. Mazzone, personal communication, March 19, 2013)

A system of relying on others supports Mazzone's ability to engage in creative work, despite the frustration it can bring.

Need for Challenge. Challenge and struggle are a part of creative processes, as is risk-taking. This is an idea that Gaines concurs with wholeheartedly. Conceiving of creativity as "a physical representation of a person's thoughts" (S. Gaines, personal communication, March 16, 2013), she believes that challenge is a crucial element in the development of important, vital skills for life in general and in creative endeavors in particular. In contrast to Mazzone, though, for Gaines, "frustration comes more from the lack of challenges than the challenges" (personal communication, March 18, 2013). Reflecting on the learning curve she navigated in her early days of knitting, she puts the idea of embracing challenge into specific context:

I've . . . been knitting since I was 16, and for a long time I avoided making socks because of how difficult [it seemed to be]. But in 2011 I realized that the only way I could get over my fear (for lack of a better word) of making socks would be to attempt to make a pair of socks, so I challenged myself, the socks ended up looking great, I gave them to my best friend for her birthday, and now socks are easy for me. (S. Gaines, personal communication, March 18, 2013)

A regard for challenge and the gifts it holds, such as growth, productivity, generative expression of ideas, and creative movement, drives Gaines as much as an absence of challenge derails her. The drive to engage challenge seems integral to her creative process, and markedly so in regard to her acting goals. She provides the following description:

If you're never challenged, you can't grow. I want to become a successful actress . . . but I need to be pushed out of my comfort zone in order to become the best actress I can be. I'm still waiting for that opportunity, and I know it'll be very intimidating once I get it, but I also know that I'll be able to take on the challenge. . . . In high school, my drama teachers were constantly telling my parents that they were afraid to push me farther because I have Asperger's syndrome, and it bothered me to hear that because I felt like they thought I couldn't do what my other classmates could do. No matter how often my parents told them that it was okay to push me farther (in fact, we all wanted them to), they wouldn't do it, and I think that lessened the experience I could have had there. I still loved my high school, and overall I had a great time, but I would have gotten more out of my drama classes if my teachers weren't so worried about pushing me. I'm very open about having Asperger's, and I want people to understand certain things that I struggle with, but I don't want anyone to think that any of those struggles limit me. (S. Gaines, personal communication, March 18, 2013)

AS plays a significant role in Gaines's comfort with discomfort. In a sense, she is in a unique bind, although one that is perhaps familiar to many autistic people. While she is committed to being open about AS (a label that came later in her life, after an early childhood classification of autism), others' perceptions about her limitations curtail her realization of the potential to be a stronger actress. The hesitation that others seem to have about pushing her too far actually disadvantages Gaines. Her identification of this problem, though, has led her to cultivate strategies for locating challenging opportunities for herself. An awareness of the strengths that accompany her vulnerabilities is at the core of her initiative to self-advocate. Gaines's earliest experiences taught her about the rift that exists between what she knows to be true of herself and what others think of her as a person with AS:

[When thinking about the word *autism*] I think of the struggles that come with having autism, and I think of how autistic people are often underestimated. People who don't have autism often focus on the difficulties that come with it without thinking about the more positive aspects. I was diagnosed when I was two, and for awhile I could only speak in other people's words (repeating what others had just said, movie quotes, etc.). But I was always really good at spelling, and I drew a lot of pictures. (S. Gaines, personal communication, March 16, 2013)

Here, Gaines illuminates the role that facets of the environment, namely, others' interpretations and attitudes, play in shaping one's ability to work toward his or her potential. While she recognizes and acknowledges her own strengths and abilities, she nonetheless conveys that her quality of life is very much influenced by the social and cultural environment in which she is engulfed. She brings to focus a very important point, which is that in order for autistic students to reach their creative potential, they need the support of school professionals in developing curricular goals that will push them in relevant ways. While Gaines navigated her school years with consistent support from her family members, who believed in her need for challenge, her experience was "lessened" in the absence of similar expectations in school.

The Importance of Home–School Collaboration. Gaines's insights prompt the idea that with strong communication between home and school and a collaborative model of goal setting, educators can support students in working toward goals that are reflective of their wishes and their families' knowledge of their abilities and needs. Both Mazzone and Gaines point out the significance of people who support them in their struggle to move beyond their current abilities. Mazzone specifically highlights how school provides a necessary structure for his development of skills and abilities in his field, and even though the demands of school often frustrate him, he has developed strategies for working through them. These insights suggest that an educational environment that initially may feel too challenging can position a person to grow through difficulty if he or she employs strategies and has the support of trusted others in the process. This is in contrast to an educational environment that provides too little challenge, where frustration can crop up as a result of boredom and idleness. Mazzone's insights highlight that when one feels in over his or her head, there are strategies that can be developed to aid progress through difficulty. When there is an absence of challenge, though, it seems far more difficult to encounter meaningful engagement and to incur growth.

Developing and Expressing Personal Voice and Perspective

Of an assigned piece he refers to as "My Sneaker" (see Figure 3.2), Mazzone notes, "The sneaker sort of represents that of Forrest Gump: 'You can tell how much a person has walked by his shoes.'" While Mazzone later concedes that his reference to the Gump quotation is an attempt to "quip," and the illustration itself does not hold much significant meaning to him, he does think of the shoe as "a 'tool' for anybody who wants to make a journey for themselves" (personal communication, June 25, 2013).

Mazzone's piece "My Sneaker" points to the reality that sometimes art is simply art. To probe for deeper meaning behind a piece of art can be in vain at times, as the drive to create a piece can be rooted in a variety of motivations such as skill practice, satisfying a class assignment, or completing a commissioned piece. However, often, art does serve as a medium to communicate values and beliefs, a reflection of life lived thus far, and a vision for a fairer future.

In the previous chapter, autism autobiographer Ido Kedar elucidates the role of creativity in the process of developing and sharing one's voice

Figure 3.2. My Sneaker

and perspective. He uses writing to process difficulties associated with autism and to discuss issues that bear significant meaning to him as a nonverbal autistic person. Further, he suggests ideas for educators' work with others who share his struggles. In this way, Kedar shows how creative action catalyzes an articulation of one's thoughts and ideas, which can reach a broad audience.

Poetry as a Forum. Similarly, through poetry, Tito Mukhopadhyay finds a forum for honing his voice and sharing his perspectives with others. He highlights how autism and creative action prove to be a unique combination in regard to developing personal perspective and voice. While he does publish his poetry, Mukhopadhyay's everyday language also portrays a poetic quality. This is exemplified several times in Biklen's *Autism and the Myth of the Person Alone* (2005). At one point, Mukhopadhyay suggests that language is overrated, asserting, "You do not need words to communicate many things, like something as subtle as assurance. Look at the setting sun. Does it need words to tell the earth that it will be back on the sky the next day?" (Mukhopadhyay & Biklen, 2005, p. 118). In another passage, Mukhopadhyay welcomes Biklen to Bangalore, assuring him, "In the market you will find India" (p. 113). His summation of the market evokes an image of a matryoshka doll, containing within its layers India's textures, sounds, fragrances, tastes, sights, and tempers. Although unreliable speech is a feature of autism for Mukhopadhyay, his agile and impressionistic strokes with language vividly mark his communication. Clearly an area of strength, language acts as a tool that he uses for exploring injustices. In conversation with Biklen, he evokes the tension inherent in having an intelligent mind and a body that will not allow him to communicate his ideas in conventional, recognizable ways:

What use is my intelligence when I heard the rubbish from the experts on Autism and yet all I could do was flap my hands, which is believed to be one of my traits? And what use is my intelligence when I hear that I am one of those idiot-savants and cannot say my words? So I have renamed myself as an intelligent junk. (p. 131)

His coining of the concept "intelligent junk" is of course an outcrop of his history. Difficulty with communication and behavioral attributes such as hand flapping prompt him to question the relevance of his perceptive mind in a world that expects verbal agility and judges based on outward appearances. In his poem "The Misfit," Mukhopadhyay (2010) conveys powerful commentary on his way of being, which has been widely questioned and regarded as inferior throughout his life.

The Misfit

There was the earth, turning and turning.
The stars receded, as if
Finding no wrong with anything.
Birds flew by all morning—
The sky lit
From the earth's turning and turning.
My hands, as usual, were flapping.
The birds knew I was Autistic;
They found no wrong with anything.
Men and women stared at my nodding;
They labeled me a Misfit
(A Misfit turning and turning).
And then I was the wind, blowing.
Did anyone see my trick?
I found no wrong with anything.
Somewhere a wish was rising,
Perhaps from between my laughing lips.
Why stop turning and turning
When right can be found with everything?

In this poem, Mukhopadhyay aligns himself with another natural entity, the earth. He questions the seemingly random way that other people accept one entity's patterns while deeming the other entity a "misfit." In poetry and in everyday communication, Mukhopadhyay engages with issues of identity and broad cultural convictions about accepted ways of being. He conveys that autism is a way of being that is concomitant with rhythms, movements, and qualities no more random or less "natural" than those of planetary bodies or atmospheric properties. Mukhopadhyay's work reveals a careful observance of nature: a setting sun, an autistic mind, or a blue sky. Simultaneously, he questions judgments that deny these to be equally acceptable "truths" of nature. In an email exchange, I asked Mukhopadhyay whether the natural environment serves to ground him, inspire him, and allow him a point of reference. He responded,

> I usually make my presence in relationship to my surroundings—be it a tree or be it a market or a rock. It is as if I have a circle around me. The radius may be as wide as a sunset or narrow as a market or still narrow as my image behind a mirror. Once I measure it, the navigation becomes easier and it puts less pressure on my senses. The boundary between me as centre and the circumference as the limit makes the concentrated attention become detailed. All I need to do is to word the details that surface in my passages. (T. Mukhopadhyay, personal communication, June 13, 2013)

In "placing" himself at the center of a given space, Mukhopadhyay stakes a point from which he can begin the articulate process of communicating his perceptions. The precise way he locates himself in space, while alleviating his senses, supports his ability to express the subtleties he observes in his environment.

His poetic responses related to the world around him reveal Mukhopadhyay's capacity to grasp and communicate with delicate nuance the intricacies of life as he knows it: the facets of India as represented in the market and the uselessness of words to communicate truths that are integral to our daily, earthly existence. His creative work is a platform with which he rebukes broad culture's deficit conceptions of his worth. Within his creative work, Mukhopadhyay reveals a point of view enlivened by sharp perceptive abilities and a manner of communicating those perceptions that is touched, in its ethereality and eloquence, by the struggles and capacities he engages.

Painting and Film as Connection. While Mukhopadhyay's poetry serves as a medium to share his observations and his voice, Bissonnette (2013) similarly sees painting as a way to give material form to his intuitions. Applying paint to canvas with his hands, Bissonnette layers colors sometimes so thick that the end result appears like a topographical map, defined by its ridges, curves, and bumps. In its tactility, painting is a form of expression that gives him a chance to share with others his "artistic voice not my autistic voice" (Synopsis, 2015). In the absence of the expectation of linguistic expression, painting represents a mode of communication that, for a nonverbal autistic person, appears to be liberating. Bissonnette separates his creative actions into the categories of artistic versus autistic expression. However, it is clear that all of his expressions are significantly marked by his connectedness to other people, as previously discussed. Throughout *Wretches and Jabberers*, Bissonnette takes Polaroid photographs of the people he meets and spends his days with. Like the Polaroid portraits that accompany his paintings, in his travels he shows appreciation for those who have impacted his life in positive ways.

While making *Wretches and Jabberers* gave Bissonnette a medium for exploring and sharing his "autistic voice," his participation in the production evidences similar qualities to those he conveys in his paintings. Although the media differ, in expressing both his *artistic* voice and his *autistic* voice, Bissonnette evidences his wit, desire to be with and appreciation for others, and desire to work through difficulties with earnest conviction.

In the film, with Thresher and their assistants, Bissonnette travels to international cities uniting with other autistic people in a quest to disrupt notions that equate nonverbal autism with a lack of intelligence. As the men discuss and reflect on their travel experiences, Bissonnette goes back to the idea that the true value of their journey resides in the meaningful connections they have forged with others who are working to carve a new narrative about autism's meanings. At one point, Bissonnette reframes a common assumption that autistic people are socially deficient, positing that the "cause of poor social skills is isolation, not lack of intelligence." This is a powerful statement, and one that has been encountered earlier in this book. It relates to a focus on practices that are common to socializing institutions such as schools, where the focus remains on remediating the supposedly "broken" individual. Bissonnette believes that "autism is not abnormality of brain as much as abnormality of experience," and thinks of autism as one of many ways of being that is as natural as any other. He observes, "Mankind expresses itself finely in variety. We are one branch of many on a long diverse and wonderful beauty tree." While autism is a way of being that plays a powerful role in shaping his life experiences, Bissonnette contends with many difficulties related to autism. Some of these difficulties appear in the film, such as his struggle to manage menacing sounds he encounters in Asian temples. In response to a resounding drum in a Sri Lankan temple, he covers his ears, paces, and makes sounds to counter the noise. Yet it appears that with time, the noises become easier for Bissonnette to bear. Later in the film, in a Japanese temple, his reaction softens: He describes the unsettling sound of a gong being struck as somehow buffered, like "dynamite wrapped in silk."

Mukhopadhyay and Bissonnette highlight how artistic engagement gives rise to and provides an outlet for personal voice and perspective. In observing how individuals use diverse styles to express their ideas, it is possible to discern how they learn, what they deem important and valuable, and what they find interesting and motivating. These are all integral qualities of personal voice and perspective. As Bissonnette demonstrates, art can give life to ideas that otherwise might go unrecognized due to, for instance, lack of agility with language or comfort with one form of communication over another. Art, then, can provide additional "languages" with which to express one's ideas.

In this way, artistic engagement offers a way to differentiate instruction that can benefit autistic students and neurotypical students alike. For any student, art can catalyze the exploration of diverse channels of communication. Poetry writing can support nontraditional uses of language and a sense of playfulness with regard to words and sentence structure. Nonlinguistic forms of art, such as painting and drawing, can push students with verbal abilities to develop alternative ways of communicating ideas. Likewise, nonlinguistic art forms can help students who lack or struggle with verbal ability to build linguistic skills, their participation and products serving as springboards for that development. This is exemplified earlier in the chapter (and will be evident later in the chapter as well) in Goldsmith's comment about how music helped strengthen his ability to access and express himself linguistically. It is likewise evident in Bissonnette's paintings and accompanying commentary.

Providing a Channel for Propensities and Enduring Interests

As discussed earlier in the book, not allowing autistic students to bring their interests into the classroom is literally asking them to leave *themselves* at home (Winter-Messiers, 2007). This sentiment highlights the imperative to meet students where they are and to acknowledge that their interests are very much tied to their self-concept. It likewise evokes the idea that a student is much more likely to learn if he or she has a vested interest in the work. Having strong attachments to personal interests appears to complement several qualities that many autistic people report sharing. Such qualities include the ability to attend intently and singularly to an area of interest, the drive to understand topics in depth, and the propensity to engage routine and gravitate toward familiarity. When coupled with systems of support, these qualities can dovetail with qualities necessary for creative development, which requires dedication and focus and thrives on novel means of expression.

Finding a channel that supports and complements one's enduring interests and propensities can give rise to different forms of expansion. Here, contributors highlight how pastimes can evolve into career paths, how "obsessions" can lead to broader interests and skills, and how negotiating what one wants to do with what trusted others want them to do can foster a sense of balance.

From Pastime to Career Path. As a looming scaffold for his interest in illustration, art school gives Mazzone an opportunity to fuse some of his inherent characteristics with his interests to meet specific, meaningful goals. Art school is likewise a forum for Mazzone: a place to showcase his work and to conceive of himself as the artist that he is and is becoming. He discusses how enrollment in art school has allowed him to formalize a lifelong love of drawing:

> Art school has been a huge impact on me because what started as a hobby turned into a way of life for me. And, it has completely changed the way I think of art in the sense of just drawing a picture. Now it's like creating your own world and trying to show others how you can create and share your ideas with them. (V. Mazzone, personal communication, June 7, 2013)

This conceptualization of art grows from Mazzone's basic understanding of creativity, which he parallels to "opening a new door and discovering a new world. Then creating a life for that world giving it existence and purpose" (V. Mazzone, personal communication, March 15, 2013).

A structural element that supports Mazzone's ability to engage creatively is the physical place in which he works. He asserts, "I work on most of my projects at home . . . it's a great benefit for me because I'm working in a place that I'm familiar with" (V. Mazzone, personal communication, June 7, 2013). Mazzone's portfolio work likewise suggests the pivotal role that familiarity of subject matter plays in his ability to move in new creative directions. For a piece he calls "Japanese-Style Watercolor of a Fisherman and Birds" (see Figure 3.3), he shares, "What inspired me to make the watercolor was thinking 'If it's watercolor why not have water?'" (V. Mazzone, personal communication, June 7, 2013). Mazzone's decision to employ a new technique, watercolor, to a painting literally focused on water has a spontaneous quality as well as a symbolic one. He shares, "The fisherman is supposed to represent peacefulness, patience, and calmness" (V. Mazzone, personal communication, June 7, 2013). The subject of the piece likewise bears reference to Mazzone's life. He notes that when time permits, he likes to go fishing in New Jersey with his father and brother.

While Mazzone's interest in illustration has led him to an educational program that formalizes his interest and helps prepare him for a future career as an artist, Mukhopadhyay engaged a different form of preparation for his career as a poet. From his mother, he learned to communicate by pointing at a letter board, and then by handwriting. The ability to write allows Mukhopadhyay to express observations of the world around him in poetic form. Objects that inhabit his surroundings are familiar and beloved muses, ones that he gives new life to in his work. Mukhopadhyay's poem "A Simple Cup" (2010) demonstrates this reality and how an "obsession" can inspire one's imagination to transform that "obsession" into a work of creativity.

Figure 3.3. Japanese-Style Watercolor of a Fisherman and Birds

A Simple Cup

Nothing could make me
stop thinking
about it.
Its inside was white
and its outside
had
some patches of colors—
orange and yellow,
randomly marked
here and there
by some one who was perhaps
entertaining his vision
with orange and yellow creation.
It lived on the kitchen shelf
like a smile,
watching all the food preparation

from the kitchen shelf.
Who knows what the smile
was about?
No one fed it anything but tea.
Nothing could stop me
from staring at its smile.
It entered my heart from the kitchen shelf
until it turned into
my obsession.
And then—
I never
wanted to leave the kitchen!
Who knows what might have
happened to the cup
forever after?
The cup, white on the inside,
patches of yellow and orange
on the outside,
turned into a memory.
It returned one dream
to begin this poem.
And ever since then,
at a moment called When,
I began my thoughts
of filling and emptying
that cup of memory—
in orange and yellow patches—
with my story.

In this poem, Mukhopadhyay gives animate qualities to a very familiar object, the teacup in his kitchen. The teacup watches, smiles, and opens its "mouth" for tea. Here, Mukhopadhyay regards a familiar object and a familiar experience with novelty, bringing the teacup to life, allowing it to go unnoticed for awhile, and then having it re-emerge again in his life. In another poem, "The Sunset Hour" (2010), Mukhopadhyay again visits familiar observations and again gives what he knows intently a new representation.

The Sunset Hour

The yolk of the sun was scrambled
By some clouds in the west.
The earth was turning purple.
Two birds sat on an electric cable,
Chatting perhaps about each other's nests,
As the light of the sun got scrambled.

The downtown seemed to tremble;
Its streets were now congested,
The pavement turning purple.
The earth looked like a confused bubble,
A floating pointlessness—
Its sun was getting scrambled.
The cars, too, seemed scrambled, their people
Rushing home—as restlessly
As the city veering into purple.
The street lamps lit up as usual,
Glowing through the darkness,
While the sun sank, all scrambled,
Into a tomb of velvet purple.

In this poem, Mukhopadhyay showcases his connection to the rhythms of daily life, both celestial and urban. A liberal use of color in his descriptions promotes the sense that he is painting a picture with words. He evokes a distinct sense of place in his attention to shades, movement, sudden yet expected changes; the turning of light into dark followed by subtle spikes of light ("The street lamps lit up as usual"); and finally a disappearance into deep darkness ("a tomb of . . . purple"). Mukhopadhyay's powers of observation, particularly of familiar surroundings, are again revealed and transformed into creative expression.

"Obsession" to Expansion. Areas of deep interest or "obsession" also play a role in broadening autistic artists' repertoire of knowledge, interests, and skills. Goldsmith shares, "The obsessive characteristic of autism has enabled me to focus on practice and becoming a better guitarist and musician" (personal communication, March 21, 2013). Being "obsessed" with music and having a preference for routine give him an internal structure by which he can practice and hone his musical skills and abilities. Goldsmith's qualities likewise position him to meet the task of mastering his musical skills with dedication. While Goldsmith's "obsessive" tendencies reinforce his ability to improve musically, he regards obsession constructively, as a quality of autism that influences his worldview. "Initially," he shares, "I thought autism was a label that meant emotional and intellectual limitations, but now I feel autism is an alternative way of living and seeing the world" (H. Goldsmith, personal communication, March 21, 2013). He elaborates on the ways that music has done more than just provide a medium through which to channel his enduring interests. Music also has given him a forum for experimenting with other media and interests, supported the development of complementary skill sets, and helped him build friendships:

Music has definitely expanded my life. It has helped me become more disciplined and patient (both from practicing the instrument and working in bands), and verbally articulate (I have learned how to express myself because of the emotional aspects of many of my favorite songs). Music has also expanded my friendships, because talking about music is my ice-breaker for meeting new people . . . it has also taught me not to be closed minded, because now I am also interested in literature, movies, paintings, and graphic novels. But music has definitely become second nature to me, I always have a rhythm playing in my head. (H. Goldsmith, personal communication, June 15, 2013)

In a similar vein, Gaines maintains an overarching and longstanding goal of performing on Broadway, but she also takes opportunities to acquire new skills and abilities that enrich her professional resources. She practices different forms of performance, integrates fresh ideas into her work, and expands her repertoire of communicative devices. A native speaker of English, Gaines earned a minor in Spanish and in addition uses American Sign Language (ASL). A clear demonstration of Gaines's interest in communicative devices is in her performance of the song "I Believe" from the musical *The Book of Mormon* in ASL (Gaines, 2013). Performing the song for a class project, Gaines provides two sets of captions along with her signing, the top line of captions corresponding to what she is literally signing, and the bottom line representing the song's lyrics. Attention to three forms of communication—signing, playing the auditory version of the song, and writing the captions—broadens the access points from which people can experience the performance. Gaines puts emphasis on the most heartfelt of lines, and her facial expressions and bodily movements fuse a depth of feeling with playful treatment of the lyrics.

Making oneself accessible to a broader swath of humanity through the development of various communicative devices seemingly positions one to find success in the performing arts. It likewise enhances one's ability to form relationships with many others. When I asked Gaines whether her learning to use ASL was in any way connected to her difficulties with language as a child, she clarified:

That never occurred to me, but it's definitely possible that my interest in ASL might have something to do with the struggles I used to have. My professor showed my class a documentary about audism (discrimination against people who are deaf or hard of hearing), and a lot of people talked about the difficulties they had and the ways people discriminated against them, sometimes without even realizing it. One person said that when she would have dinner with her family, she didn't feel included in the conversations because everyone else was hearing. When she asked what was going on, people would tell her not to worry about it or that they'd explain later. She didn't want someone to explain later; she wanted her family to include her. I've had to deal with the phrase, "I'll explain later," or people just assuming that I wouldn't understand, so even though I've never had difficulty hearing, I was able to relate to some of their struggles. (S. Gaines, personal communication, September 4, 2013)

A general ability to relate to the struggles of other people, while not necessarily due to her early difficulties with language, aids Gaines in expanding the ways in which she can reach and communicate with others.

Balancing on a Tightrope. The investments that Gaines puts into her work as a performance artist are ones that she anticipates reaping benefits from well into her future. Other day-to-day forms of creative engagement likewise have given her a constructive outlet for her propensity to commit to a goal and attack it with sheer practice. This, she describes, is a quality that unites her with so many other autistic people:

I think my ability to stick to one creative outlet, as opposed to abandoning things and picking something new every week, played a lot into my development . . . instead of learning a bunch of things and getting pretty good at all of them, I stuck with one or two things at a time and became really good at those things. . . . From what I've experienced, a lot of people on the autistic spectrum become great at a specific type of creativity, and that's because they focus on it a lot. When I was younger I was always drawing, and now I spend most of my spare time knitting or crocheting. People comment on how good I am at knitting and crocheting, and I appreciate the compliments, but the reason I've become so good at it is that I stuck with it and kept practicing. I've noticed a lot that when people on the autistic spectrum become interested in something, they get very into it and stick with that interest for a long time, and that allows their creativity to shine through in the best way possible. (S. Gaines, personal communication, March 16, 2013)

Here, Gaines suggests that given a structure for practicing and sharpening skills and abilities, autistic people can exercise their deep interests toward constructive ends and moreover can realize a sense of fulfillment and satisfaction in developing their potential. Her experiences have taught her the importance of scaffolding autistic students' ability to engage their interests in a way that is generative and meaningful. Speaking from the perspective of teaching autistic students, Gaines shares,

I think focusing so much on one thing can be thought of as negative for people who don't fully understand the autistic spectrum, and in a way I understand that. I volunteered at [a school for autistic students] during the summer of 2011 and I had students that talked and thought about the same things all the time (shoes, popular singers, etc.). I often had to get them to stop talking about those things and focus on whatever we were doing, but at the same time I think that if someone discovers a talent, they should be encouraged to embrace that talent. I do think it's important to help people think about other things, but I think we should do that without taking the things they're passionate about away from them. (personal communication, March 16, 2013)

Levering one's passions and interests with the introduction of new, less well-loved topics is thus the key, in Gaines's estimation, to readying oneself to meet the many demands that creative work, and life, inevitably bring. With practical sensibility, Gaines seems to have approached the task of walking a tightrope, which so many autistic people report to struggle with: that fine line between attending to what one wants to do and what others deem necessary or important. There are many contextual features that have enhanced Gaines's ability to engage her interests constructively, including: the chance to study and practice her craft(s) since early adolescence, the many supportive people in her life such as her parents and friends, the opportunity to attend public schools with diverse peers, and growing up in a city that is in and of itself rich in resources for expanding her knowledge of theater and performing arts. Qualities such as a desire to hone skills before moving on to other subjects, a drive to reach others via diverse communicative devices, and a willingness to be open about AS and what it means for her likewise help Gaines navigate the difficult path of attending to her wishes while considering the relevance of the wishes of others.

PROSPECTS FOR SKILL AND ABILITY
BUILDING THROUGH THE ARTS

As the artists featured in this chapter attest, the prospects for skill and ability building through arts-based creative work are many. It is not difficult to imagine how their insights about artistic engagement can transfer to classrooms and schools. The artists share how artistic engagement can strengthen a community in which each individual learns to stretch his or her capacities in new ways and learns from and with diverse peers about alternative ways of seeing and being in the world. For the information that is revealed about one's propensities, struggles, strengths, and interests in the process, and for the abilities that it catalyzes, artistic engagement holds value for students, educators, and classroom communities as a whole.

The artists expose how skills developed through arts-based creative work are technical, linguistic, intrapersonal, interpersonal, and communicative in nature. With regard to classroom application, enfolding arts-based work allows for personal perspectives to develop and shine, binds one to a world broader than one's own, improves tactile skills, reinforces a relationship between body and mind, and forges connections between seemingly disparate topics and people. Further, engaging in arts-based creative work introduces the opportunity to move through struggle and to embrace challenge in efforts to grow beyond one's current abilities and zones of comfort. In an atmosphere of openness to difference, arts-based work can build classroom communities and illuminate how diversity strengthens and enriches a community in which each member contributes her or his novel form of expression.

CHAPTER 4

Educators' Role in Cultivating Creative Learning in Autistic Students

Very often, creativity is thought to be games and strategies that are done in isolation of core subject matter, but this is a misconception.

—Alexinia Young Baldwin (2010)

The previous chapters have demonstrated how creativity can be found in a number of contexts and have focused on what creativity reveals and what it catalyzes. Imaginative and creative thinking and action are evident in everyday communication, in responses to circumstantial challenges, in writing, and in arts-based work.

In this chapter, I focus on ways that educators can attend to and integrate strategies for encouraging autistic students' creative engagement and growth. The ideas shared in this chapter emphasize flexibility in curricular and instructional adaptation and are relevant to autistic students in grades K–12 who represent verbal and nonverbal communicative abilities. However, as Baldwin's (2010) words above evoke, these ideas also point to a new way of thinking about educating all students for an age of innovation. Beyond differentiating curricula and instruction for diverse student needs, the focus here is on integrating ways to teach for creative thinking and to immerse students in the processes of creative action. This approach unites all students, as each engages in creative action every single day. Several actions can help educators set the stage for teaching for creativity. Thinking through ways to engage all members of a learning community is a critical step in providing an inclusive environment that invites and anticipates the perspectives of all students. Making accessible to all class members strategies that are particularly useful for autistic youth (e.g., preteaching, visual components, extended time or space to process ideas) gives each the chance to develop his or her creative abilities through diverse methods of learning, participating, and expressing. This chapter weaves creativity research into a discussion of several topics that are significant for supporting autistic students' creative abilities: teaching for a creative age, laying a foundation for creativity and inclusion, providing systems of support, offering appropriate challenges, channeling and developing interests in constructive ways, and enabling means of expression.

TEACHING FOR A CREATIVE AGE

The development of everyday creativity is at the forefront of contemporary scholarship on creativity and education. This vein of research argues for the importance of helping every student realize his or her creative potential. Sawyer (2010) notes how traditional schooling is based on an industrial model that was designed to prepare the majority of youth for industrial era jobs (i.e., factory work). This type of schooling prioritizes conformity and fails to reflect contemporary cultural shifts and needs. In the current era, often referred to as the "creative age" (p. 176), there is a global need to prepare citizens for the ability to innovate, which requires creative- and critical-thinking skills. Sawyer provides a compelling argument that in order for schools to truly integrate creative-thinking ability, major educational reform will be needed. Schools, he notes, must reflect the cultural shift that now represents a need for deep, as opposed to superficial, knowledge of ideas and concepts. Students furthermore must be able to understand ideas and concepts in more holistic ways, across multiple contexts. In schools that reflect this cultural shift, Sawyer notes, "creativity will be suffused throughout the curriculum" (p. 176). This contrasts with the way that creative learning historically has been the provenance of arts-based classes.

Understanding creativity as a quality that touches all of our lives, daily, is an important element of moving toward new educational models such as that discussed by Sawyer. Musician and creativity scholar Nachmanovitch (1990) believes that creativity is enacted at the very basic level of linguistic expression, which he suggests is one of humanity's most conspicuous forms of creative improvisation. Nachmanovitch explains how the interplay of cultural norms and personal expressive choices works in tandem to create linguistic novelty. He comments,

> The most common form of improvisation is ordinary speech. As we talk and listen, we are drawing on a set of building blocks (vocabulary) and rules for combining them (grammar). These have been given to us by our culture. But the sentences we make with them may never have been said before and may never be said again. Every conversation is a form of jazz. The activity of instantaneous creation is as ordinary to us as breathing. (p. 17)

While Nachmanovitch's conception of linguistic expression as "as ordinary to us as breathing" refers to speech, it is clear that other forms of linguistic expression likewise evidence creativity. Mukhopadhyay's poetic quality of language and Bissonnette's unconventional linguistic constructions reflect qualities of improvisation and prompt a moment to pause and reread their words, in an effort to discern their meanings. Autistic expression, again, can represent new ways of using and perceiving language and beckons attention to the ways that bodily orientation, proprioceptive reality, or neurological features can play a role in the quality of one's linguistic expression (see Savarese, 2008). All students can benefit from exposure to autistic perspectives in curricular experiences.

LAYING A FOUNDATION FOR CREATIVITY AND INCLUSION

The importance of environment in the cultivation of creative ability is emphasized commonly among creativity scholars and is evoked by the autistic people represented in this book. Classrooms that foster students' ability to think flexibly, in both divergent and convergent ways, prepare students for real-world creative endeavors.

Educational environments that value and model an attitude of openness to possibilities and stress the idea that there are multiple solutions to a given problem encourage divergent thinking (Fairweather & Cramond, 2010). Divergent thinking is important for piquing and developing imagination, and it allows students to play with ideas, brainstorm, and consider a variety of solutions to a problem before articulating a plan for solving the problem. Convergent thinking, on the other hand, is a process of narrowing down possibilities.

Most contemporary creativity scholars suggest that each of these types of thinking is important, at given times, for creative ability building (Sawyer, 2010). Convergent thinking is necessary for success on conventional standardized tests, where there is one answer deemed to be correct. Yet this type of thinking also does have a place in creative development. For example, convergent thinking is useful at points in creative processes when individuals must make judgments about which possibilities to pursue or abandon.

Some creativity scholars (e.g., Baer & Garrett, 2010) suggest that creative learning be focused on domain-specific activities, and this idea dovetails with what many autistic people featured in this book have suggested. Enabling students to fuse their interests and deep knowledge of those areas with curricular activities that expand their creative thinking holds the promise of enhancing students' meaningful engagement in school, provided other supports are attended to.

Other creativity scholars (e.g., Beghetto & Kaufman, 2010; Richards, 2010), however, emphasize the importance of integrating creative-thinking habits across all subject domains, with a focus on everyday forms of creativity that are relevant to all people. Such a focus would highlight qualities of resourcefulness, working within constraints, turning problems on their head in order to stimulate novel approaches and solutions, and cultivating a sense of newness to familiar problems. In this type of teaching for creativity, students are assumed to engage creatively each time they locate a novel solution to a problem. Creativity scholar Boden (2004) refers to this type of creativity as psychological or "P" creativity and notes that while the idea may not be new to others, the fact that it is new to an individual student bears significance to his or her creative development.

Both forms of teaching for creative development are relevant and beneficial for classrooms that include autistic students. While emphasizing domain-specific creativity seems like a seamless fit for those who have intense interests in a particular area, the habits of mind cultivated by integrating creative thinking across subject matters can help autistic students to:

- Broaden their range of interests
- Recognize that many of the things they are already doing are creative acts (such as responding resourcefully to a problem)
- See connections between apparently disparate subjects
- Hone their creative sensibilities in more general ways

It is possible to attend to both types of creative teaching with autistic students' interests in mind, however. In any domain of knowledge, students can integrate their interests by use of cross-fertilization across subject areas (Sternberg, 2010), as discussed later in the chapter. That is, they can apply their areas of strength to address areas they find less inherently interesting.

In developing strategies and practices to promote student engagement in creative work, educators can be guided by the insights shared by autistic individuals in Chapters 2 and 3. That is, teachers should provide systems of support, appropriate challenges, constructive channels for interests, and means of expression. Each of these approaches appears to be integral to the creative lives and development of autistic students, as well as their neurotypical peers, and will be discussed in more detail in the rest of the chapter.

PROVIDING SYSTEMS OF SUPPORT

Many of the ideas that contemporary creativity scholars address as crucial to the cultivation of a creative learning environment evoke a sense of inclusiveness and universal relevance. Teacher practices that contribute to the support of autistic students' creative development and quality of life in school include attending to difference, validating dependence and community, participating in home–school collaboration, and providing time and space to respond to problems and work through ideas.

Attention to Difference

The insights of the autistic people featured in this book push some of the ideas expressed by creativity scholars a bit further. They suggest, for example, that an *expectation* of difference, rather than a sense of openness to difference, is integral to a community that values creativity in diverse forms. The difference is subtle yet worthy of distinction. If educators expect and plan for students of diverse abilities and ways of being in their communities, they can be thoughtful in their preparation of discussions and activities that promote a sense of inclusiveness. Their actions can be deliberate rather than reactive and can set a tone and precedent for the community as a whole. While educators can plan for expected difference among the members of their classrooms, so too can administrators help prepare teachers and support staff with necessary tools for cultivating equitable learning spaces. Professional development that integrates the voices of autistic people with regard to elements that support or hinder their ability to learn in a way qualitatively on par with their peers sets the tone for an atmosphere of openness and expectation of difference.

Ongoing observation of and conferring with students, including their nonverbal actions, can give educators information about students' propensities and personalities. Emily's sense of playfulness in her nonverbal communication comes to mind here (see Chapter 2). Illuminating through class discussions how students act and communicate in diverse ways can encourage classmates to broaden their ideas about what meaningful communication is, and send the message that diverse styles of communication are both valued and expected. Teachers also can emphasize in these discussions how diverse ways of being constitute novelty, which is a crucial element of creative thinking. Understanding that nonconventional forms of behavior are valuable to the person who demonstrates them, as well as for his or her community of learners, can strengthen the community's sense of trust. Security and trust often are cited as elements of educational communities that support students' creative risk-taking (e.g., Fairweather & Cramond, 2010), so teachers who find ways to validate students' differences can contribute to a strong foundation for creative development.

Dependence and Community

The insights of autistic individuals in this book also evoke the idea that learning communities are strengthened when there is an expectation of relevant dependence. Creativity scholars note the role of collaboration in promoting creative development within classrooms. Yet within a classroom that includes autistic students, many of whom benefit from or need the support of others to succeed in school, this imperative seems especially significant. Discussing how dependence is a quality of life that we all rely on in many ways not immediately apparent (and making those ways apparent to students) can help students understand its significance to the lives of peers who may rely in more conspicuous ways on others to traverse daily life. Teachers might point out how, for example, as a culture we have become dependent on applications such as spell-check when using word processing programs, or turning to Wikipedia or Google to access information. Then a connection can be made to a paraprofessional supporting the in-class learning of an autistic student or to the use of a letter board or other technological device to support communication and focus.

An exploration of the ways in which dependence is an integral part of life can segue into an exploration of the importance of collaboration with others to support creative development. This is not to say that all school projects and aspects of the creative process and projects must be carried out in collaboration with others. In fact, Cain (2012) discusses how studies have illuminated the very important role that solitude plays in creative development. She notes the importance of allowing quieter students ways to contribute their ideas, which often are deeply considered, in ways that are a good fit for their temperaments. Offering students the chance to contribute ideas via an online dialogue, for instance, gives quieter students a chance to reflect and contribute in a way that alleviates pressure or anxiety associated with speaking to a larger group. Excellent insights, Cain emphasizes, frequently are not shared with larger groupings because quieter students often need different participatory structures in order to feel safe sharing their thoughts. While independence is important to encourage many students to process and realize their ideas, teachers can highlight how independent work can enrich and strengthen the quality of their collaborative work. He or she can further point out that even when individuals work independently, they are not truly alone with their ideas. For one thing, creative expression builds on the knowledge of those who have come before. Further, an individual typically works with an audience in mind and shares a creation with a broader community. A teacher can build elements of healthy dependence into a classroom community by integrating diverse participation structures. Examples include partnerships, small groups, and technology to enhance students' ability to develop and share their ideas with the community in ways that align with their communicative ability, preferences, and needs.

Peer tutoring and mentor matching are other types of supports that reinforce constructive dependencies. These types of supports work best when they represent interdependencies, where each member of the collaborative effort gains benefits, or when the pair works toward common goals. When all members of the class have access to and regularly use peer tutoring and mentor matching, these structures can move beyond a primary motivation of benevolence that often characterizes peer work between disabled and nondisabled students (Jorgensen, 2006). In peer tutoring, older peers or those who have deeper knowledge of a subject area can work with students who are either younger or less versed in the subject area. In high school, I remember when my Spanish teacher paired me with an honors-level classmate to help improve my Spanish conversation skills. It felt natural and effective to learn from someone who was my own age yet had more sophisticated and fluent Spanish-speaking skills than I had. With the formal dynamic of teacher–student removed, my classmate and I worked in a relaxed way, and I remember both of us laughing a lot. This dynamic benefits both parties. The peer tutor can gain class credit or extra credit either in pedagogy or in the particular topic being tutored. Thus, the role can be rewarding in and of itself, for example, as a way for a likely hard-working student to be recognized for his or her efforts. Being asked to teach others what one knows can be a high compliment. The tutored student benefits from learning from a peer in a way that feels less formal and more relatable, and he or she can benefit from the sustained nature of the relationship.

Mentor matching can be guided by matching students with common interests, goals, and activities. Younger students (for instance, those in grades K–2) or those with less developed skills can learn from those who are a few years older (e.g., those in grades 3–5) or more knowledgeable in the area of interest. The mentor learns by having to teach his or her mentee what he or she knows, while the mentee gains valuable skills and knowledge from his or her mentor. A mentor-matching dynamic can be developed outside of school, in places such as music studios (or garages), art studios, homes, parks, playgrounds, libraries, museums, community centers, and computer, science, or photo labs.

With regard to autistic youth, peer tutoring and mentor matching are much more likely to succeed when an adult facilitator is involved to help the members navigate different stages of the tutoring dynamic or mentorship and to help support communication between the participants (Jorgensen, 2006). The facilitator could be, for example, a teacher, therapist or counselor, administrator, community volunteer or docent, parent, grandparent, or other caregiver.

For many autistic individuals, the camaraderie of other autistic people is an element of support that is indispensable. For example, in Chapter 3 Vincent Mazzone talked about the strength he maintains through his "group" made up of other autistic young adults, with whom he meets regularly. In his book, Ido Kedar refers to close autistic friends who are likewise nonverbal. These types of supportive relationships, which also are represented in online forums and advocacy groups such as the Autism

Self-Advocacy Network, can connect autistic youth with others who share common difficulties, joys, perceptions, and ways of experiencing the world. Teachers can work with families to help autistic students find and connect to one another, by locating online communities and initiating and facilitating extracurricular gatherings, collaborations, and, for very young students, play dates.

Home–School Collaboration

In Chapters 2 and 3, autistic individuals suggest the importance of strong collaboration between home and school to achieve their meaningful educational experiences. Kedar (2012) makes reference to the immense validation he felt when educators actually listened to and believed his mother's contention that his ability to communicate far surpassed what he had been told he was capable of (namely, by his ABA teachers). He likewise considers his teacher, Soma Mukhopadhyay, a "raft" (p. 97), referring to the way she believed in his potential to communicate, an act that changed his life in a profound way. In Chapter 3, Sarah Gaines discusses how she wished her high school teachers had heeded her parents' and her own desire that she be pushed and held to higher expectations in school. These insights suggest that home–school collaboration has the potential to create curricular experiences that pose enough challenge for students to incur growth and avoid stagnation, and bring clarity to specific student needs for thriving in school. Meeting such needs might entail establishing a quiet space in which to retreat for processing ideas or mitigating overwhelming stimuli, or providing preteaching materials that allow a student to gain familiarity with a given topic prior to its presentation to the whole class. Home–school collaboration furthermore can give parents or caregivers the opportunity to share their perspectives on a student's propensities, wishes, and particular habits or behaviors.

Relatedly, collaboration between home and school can give parents or caregivers the chance to share strategies that successfully and meaningfully engage their autistic student at home, as well as allowing both parents/caregivers and teachers the opportunity to discuss ways to support an autistic student through potentially difficult circumstances or emotions. As a classroom teacher, I found value in home–school collaboration as a means to fortify my ability to advocate on behalf of my students, especially when it came time to write letters of recommendation for entrance into new schools. Knowing a student not only from one's own perspective but also from the perspective of the family's values and goals for the child culminates in a holistic picture of the student. Understanding students in this way can help teachers articulate recommendations based on a number of knowledge sources.

Time and Space

Many of the people featured in this book have shared how they benefit from space and time to process, think, and contribute their best responses and work. In Chapter 2, Lucy Blackman shares how her long process of articulating a response to a class discussion is an incredibly difficult element of her learning experiences. She notes that as a student, she benefitted from being given the freedom to walk the halls to process her thoughts. In that same chapter, Alberto Frugone demonstrates a novel solution to his desire for more independence. Over time, with his mother, he brainstormed several ideas before finding a way that would allow him to remain home while his mother carried out her errands. Mazzone, in Chapter 3, shares how the physical space in which he works makes a difference in his ability to use his time constructively. He works from home to complete most of his art school projects because the familiarity (and routine) supports his ability to focus.

Time for processing ideas and working on projects is likewise noted in creativity scholarship to be an important element of creative learning communities. Amabile, Hadley, and Kramer (2002) contend that creativity is best engaged in low-pressure circumstances where long strands of time are given to a task. Similarly, in his work with legendary creative contributors, Csikszentmihalyi (1997) says that the maturation of ideas plays an important role in the development of profoundly creative contributions. Amabile and colleagues observe in their research on workplace creativity that while sustained periods of exploration with ideas is a critical element in creative problem solving, so too is the clarity and meaningfulness of the task to those doing the work. These studies support the idea that fusing a student's interests with curricular work breeds relevance, and the studies' applicability to classroom work is not a stretch. Coupled with the stated need of many autistic people for space and time to process and develop their ideas, there is a clear imperative for teachers to attend to students' interests to support their chances of putting their best work forth.

OFFERING APPROPRIATE CHALLENGES

The strong statement of Gaines about the role of challenge in the development of creative potential underscores how autistic students, regardless of the difficulties they may face, benefit from being held to high expectations on par with their neurotypical peers. Higher expectations would have given Gaines more room to grow. On the other hand, Mazzone, who experiences high expectations in art school, routinely encounters deep frustration. His struggle with challenge highlights the very useful strategies and tools he has developed in order to process and traverse frustration and self-doubt. While challenge may not always feel comfortable, with supports autistic students can gain valuable, highly transferable life skills.

Joint Goal Setting

When teachers learn about their students through observation, work samples, one-on-one conferencing, and home–school collaboration, they are positioned to enter a conversation with their students about curricular goals that reflect the students' interests, propensities, and needs. Joint goal setting is a powerful way to construct challenging curricular goals that students find inherently worthwhile and conducive to deepening and expanding their knowledge and abilities.

In his work with Emily (see Chapter 2), Linneman (2001) constructed learning goals for her through discussion with her mother and through his interactions with Emily. With a focus on supporting her advancement of computer skills, the goals reflected Emily's wishes, propensities, and needs, which she communicated through limited speech, many gestures, and other nonverbal signals. This is an example of how goal setting between teachers and students can strengthen trust and a sense of collaboration. As a special education classroom teacher, I too relied on weekly goal setting with each of my students. On Mondays, my team and I would take time to confer with students individually to articulate two to four personal goals (e.g., relating to frustration management strategies) on which each would focus for the week. Throughout the day (usually twice), we would rotate to check in with students about their goals and discuss ways to help them meet those goals if they were having trouble doing so. The process was effective because students were in charge of identifying goals that they wanted to work on in efforts to make their classroom experiences more meaningful and, often, less wrought with emotions that hindered their ability to do meaningful work. Teachers were there to facilitate and to suggest ideas for goals if students felt stuck identifying goals on their own.

While my teaching team used goal setting typically for helping students mitigate frustration and other difficult emotions, this strategy also can be used for curricular goals. Regardless of how it is used, joint goal setting is rewarding for all. Teachers can be sure that students are advancing their knowledge and skills base, and students know that their voices are being heard and that they have choice in matters related to their educational lives. Importantly, joint goal setting can address students' needs at different phases of their educational lives. In the secondary years, for instance, teachers can integrate goals that support students' preparation for the transition to college, jobs, and possibly living away from family and known routines and structures.

Individualized Education Plan

The individualized education plan (IEP) provides an opportunity for educators to formally envision a student's educational development and to advocate for curricular goals that represent appropriate challenge. It is a place where educators can address goals related to creative development and note strategies for that development. While IEPs typically are written collaboratively with input from a team of educators, they can reflect the goals articulated in teacher–student joint goal setting, where relevant. Such IEP goals could include strategies and content, highlighting how students' preferred learning styles and participatory structures support their learning of particular subjects. They likewise can include ways to creatively infuse students' interests into and across curricular learning and standards, and address plans for upcoming transitions.

Management of Obstacles and Ambiguity

Mistakes are a crucial element of creativity and, as Temple Grandin suggested in Chapter 2, serve to cultivate qualities of resourcefulness, analytical thinking, and mind–body connection. While making mistakes is a part of the creative process, so too is a related quality, having a tolerance for ambiguity. Creativity scholar Sternberg (2010) says,

> At some point everyone makes a mistake in choosing a project or in the method they select to complete it. Teachers and parents should remember that an important part of creativity is the analytical part—learning to recognize a mistake—and give students the chance and the opportunity to redefine their choices. (p. 403)

Mistakes offer students the opportunity to rethink, redirect, and refine their plans of action, yet some students may need help figuring out how to understand this perspective on mistake making. Teachers can offer ways for students to manage frustration and other emotions that are part and parcel of mistake making. The idea that mistakes are an unavoidable part of the creative process can be at the forefront of building a classroom community that values creative thinking. By promoting a tolerance for ambiguity within the classroom community, teachers can lay the groundwork for learning to mitigate difficult emotions associated with making mistakes. Learning to expect that solutions to problems might take time to realize helps students learn how to delay gratification and become increasingly comfortable with working through periods of uncertainty.

Teachers can model a tolerance for ambiguity in real-life situations within the classroom as they organically arise. An example of such a scenario might be: A kindergarten teacher receives a message that the school bus he or she requested may or may not be available to transport the class on an upcoming field trip. The class will need to wait until the day before the scheduled trip to find out whether the bus will be available or they will need to travel to their destination by alternative means. In this scenario, the teacher can share his or her frustration (e.g., via verbal or/and bodily expression), solicit different alternatives for getting to the field-trip destination, and let the students know that he or she will prepare for the worst outcome (not getting a bus) by sending home a note to parents. In the note, the teacher can ask for parent volunteers to drive in case the bus will not be available. In taking these steps, the teacher models constructive expression of frustration, openness to new approaches, and taking action toward a possible solution.

Teachers likewise can reflect on periods of their lives when they had to navigate uncertainty, with everyday concerns or with creative pursuits, and share such stories with the class. Further, to highlight the role of tolerance for ambiguity in the lives of creative people, teachers can read passages from literature such as biography, autobiography, research, fiction, journalism, or poetry, or play audio or film clips, that demonstrate how those individuals proceeded through periods of uncertainty. Using these activities as a springboard, teachers can facilitate students' sharing of times in life when they were required to delay gratification or tolerate ambiguity before realizing an outcome or goal.

In efforts to help students develop the tools necessary to manage difficult emotions that come with ambiguity and mistake making, teachers might conduct a class-wide brainstorming session on ways to manage such emotions, offering varying participation structures to encourage expression of multiple perspectives. Such structural variation could include beginning with paired or small-group discussion, or a short period of writing or typing ideas before bringing the class together to share them. It likewise (or alternatively) could take the form of a prelearning activity, where the class is assigned to think through ideas a few days before the class-wide brainstorming. To accommodate students who do better when they are able to contribute their ideas from the familiarity of their own homes, the brainstorming session could even take place online, using a program such as Blackboard or a classroom-specific portal.

Including the perspectives of people with disabilities can enrich discussions on mistake making and tolerating ambiguity. In a class that includes autistic students, teachers can select writings or film clips created by autistic people to demonstrate the particular difficulties they experience due to specific disabilities, bodily experiences, or dispositions. Alternatively, teachers can invite an autistic individual (or individuals) who works in a profession that requires a tolerance for ambiguity and making mistakes to share his or her experiences with the class. Students could prepare for the guest presenter by developing questions in advance of the visit and could even hand in the questions early so that the teacher could present the guest with the questions several days prior to the scheduled visit. If the autistic professional would prefer, the class alternatively could engage in an online discussion with him or her on the topic, which is a choice that could provide more flexibility for both the professional and the students.

Cross-Fertilization Across Subject Areas

As mentioned earlier in this chapter, cross-fertilization across subject areas (Sternberg, 2010) can help educators provide adequate and relevant challenge to their autistic students. This idea is compatible with thematic units, where subject areas that traditionally are regarded as discrete (e.g., math, social studies, physical education) are explored within a common theme (e.g., community, mapping, the Westward Movement). Approaching curricula in a thematic way helps students recognize connections between seemingly disparate subjects, promotes a sense of relevance since subjects can be understood within diverse contexts and from different perspectives, and can support students' ability to learn about a particular theme in depth. Exploring subjects in this way can help students transfer their knowledge to other learning experiences as well, as they come to view learning as a process of interconnecting information as opposed to a process of compartmentalizing knowledge.

Facilitating an understanding of learning that underscores interconnectedness between subject areas fortifies creative thinking. From Sternberg's (2010) perspective, cross-fertilization of subjects means tapping students' strengths in the name of relevant and meaningful learning. He shares, "Teaching students to cross-fertilize draws on their skills, interests, and abilities, regardless of the subject" (p. 410), and notes that cross-fertilization appeals particularly to students who have deep area(s) of interest and who value concrete (as opposed to abstract) learning. He provides an example: "Teachers can explain to students that they can apply their interest in science to social studies by analyzing the scientific aspects of trends in national politics" (p. 410). Bridging an area of familiarity with areas of unfamiliarity breeds the development of new insights. Encouraging cross-fertilization sets the stage for creativity because students are positioned to make links between areas they might never have aligned in the past. Novel ideas that emerge from cross-fertilization of subject areas represent a form of creativity that people encounter in everyday life, yet conventional schooling has focused on treating subjects as necessarily distinct.

In Chapter 3, when Henry Goldsmith describes the role that music has played in his life, he highlights how musical expression opened him up to appreciate a host of other expressive forms: paintings, literature, movies, and graphic novels. In doing so, he demonstrates the significance and relevance of cross-fertilization of subjects in real-world contexts. Expression in the form of music has enriched Goldsmith's quality of life not only by connecting him to new communities of people, but also by providing him with opportunities for learning about seemingly distinct expressive modalities.

CHANNELING AND DEVELOPING INTERESTS IN CONSTRUCTIVE WAYS

In Chapter 2, Grandin illuminates the importance of finding constructive routes for autistic youth to channel their impulses toward particular subject areas and interests. She notes how hands-on training that was once ubiquitous in schools is now gone and that classes like home economics, textiles, metal shop, and auto mechanics once gave students the chance to explore a mind–body connection. These types of activities allow for experimentation, learning through trial and error, and skill building in a specific area. Tactile learning likewise helps students develop concrete, useful, practical abilities that can bolster their job readiness and appeal to potential employers in various fields. Grandin fears that modern habits, such as a push to engage technological over tactile learning, are promoting a glut of knowledgeable citizens who have little to offer the job market in the way of practical skill sets. Her concern for youth on the autism spectrum is a response to her observation that so many of these youth often become absorbed in computer and video games. Although these youth become knowledgeable in these areas, she notes that they too often end up underemployed. Tactile learning experiences can give these youth an additional layer of knowledge and experience and contribute to a more dynamic profile of skills.

Her insights are important. While it is imperative that interests and strengths be at the center of facilitating autistic students' learning, it is likewise critical to ensure that learning prepares them for a range of real-world jobs and experiences. Autistic students are not the only ones who stand to gain from the reintroduction of tactile learning experiences in school. An emphasis on abstract learning can lead to a deprivation of concrete learning experiences, and many students feel a pull to engage in crafts, cooking, weaving, and other forms of hands-on skill building. Engagement with a variety of materials and modalities of expression is important for all students, throughout their school careers. In addition to offering the tactile learning experience suggested by Grandin (which she seems to gear toward secondary students), there are several features that classroom teachers can attend to that will support autistic students' dynamic preparation for life beyond school.

Class-Wide Exploration of Student Interests

To underscore the value and significance of integrating interests and strengths into curricular learning, teachers can conduct a class-wide exploration of each student's interests and strengths. As an example, the exploration might take the form of posters that 2nd-graders make highlighting the things they like and attributes of themselves that they think are their strong points (e.g., a version of "All About Me" posters). Based on interests and/or strengths, students could be grouped together, where a deeper exploration of the shared qualities can be facilitated. Such groupings should be diverse in terms of experience, ability, and knowledge, with students joined together by virtue of a shared love of, for example, bike riding, domestic animals, or trains. (Teachers may need to get creative with groupings, perhaps broadening certain themes. For instance, they may need to include a variety of transportation vehicles in a grouping if only a few students show an interest in cars, or airplanes, or trains. Alternatively, smaller groupings or pairs could lead to a deeper study of a topic.)

An older class could use interests or strengths to guide groupings for collaborative work projects, such as a study of the cardiovascular system. A class of high school students could brainstorm possible approaches or angles from which to engage the study, and formulate groupings made up of members whose knowledge and skills would benefit the pursuit of particular approaches or angles.

The idea is to showcase or demonstrate that each community member has unique strengths and special interests yet also has the potential to unite with others who share those or similar qualities. The project can help students realize the importance of interests and strengths in connecting with others and in doing meaningful work. This realization is an important foundation for building a learning community that values the integration of all members' interests and strengths.

Attention to Propensities When Planning Instruction

All students have preferred ways of participating and engaging in learning, and these propensities can be attended to at the planning level. Through many of the means already discussed in this chapter (home–school collaboration, observation, IEP collaboration), teachers can get to know their students' propensities. Then teachers can plan instruction and curricula with the diverse needs of their classroom in mind to make learning experiences accessible to all students. Instruction can offer a range of accessibility points, such as:

- Discussions (pairs, groups, whole class)
- Visual demonstration
- Auditory demonstration (e.g., listening to an audio clip of a historical figure giving a speech or an interview)
- Tactile exploration
- Computer-based exploration (where students access the information individually or in pairs)
- Reading material
- Any combination of the above

While this list does not constitute all possible access points for instruction, it indicates that there are as many access points (and more) as there are diverse student propensities.

Some students' propensities for optimum learning situations may require environmental modifications, such as the following:

- Specific spaces in which to work
- Quiet areas in which to retreat when overwhelmed with sensory stimulation
- Headphones or sound buffers (see Bissonnette's experience in the Asian temples in Chapter 3)
- The freedom to leave the room if necessary to process thoughts (as Blackman needed; see Chapter 3)

These options come with the expectation that there is always a place for the student when he or she feels ready to return to the class activity. Further, teachers can allow for movement when students struggle to sit still during more passive periods, such as during discussions or listening to audio recordings. Movement can help many students maintain focus. And while many autistic people report a sense of annoyance with their "stims" such as hand-flapping, an atmosphere of acceptance of diverse ways of processing emotion or sensation conveys that movements, even the unconventional, are part of the learning and creative process.

Dynamic Engagement in Class Projects

The curriculum approach of cross-fertilization of subjects, discussed above, is particularly suitable for autistic students, who represent a diversity of participatory preferences and often have deep areas of interest. Teachers can use cross-fertilization strategies to help autistic students engage curricular material dynamically, as they expand their repertoire of knowledge, creatively link disparate subjects, and build social and communication skills. Each of these abilities is valuable for the world beyond the classroom.

Here is an example of the way strengths and interests can guide rich curricular work. Teachers can facilitate partnerships between nonverbal autistic students and speaking peers, who can share their written or typed insights and perceptions. An autistic student with an interest in animation but little interest in economics nonetheless is required to complete a project for her U.S. economics class. This student can use her interest in animation to guide her work by conducting an investigation of the way that animation has contributed to the financial strength of the entertainment industry. She could focus on a mainstream animator, such as Disney or Pixar, then diverge from the mainstream animator to compare and contrast a smaller animator's role in the overall financial health of the industry. Presentation of the student's ideas might take various forms, such as a poster project, a computer-based demonstration, a piece of animation, or a written paper. With support from a speaking peer or talking software, the student can present her ideas on a par with her classmates.

Investigation of Potential Jobs and Careers

Teachers can facilitate autistic students' exploration of potential career paths. Beginning the exploration early (such as in the late elementary years) leaves time for gathering information, exposure to a variety of materials and resources, and ample experimentation with possible options. One way of exposing students to potential career paths is to bring in guest speakers who represent a variety of fields (educators can reference the interests of their particular student body to discern whom to invite). Reading biographies or watching documentaries or films about the lives of prominent people in one's field of interest is another way to promote exposure to diverse careers. Likewise, locating exemplars of autistic people who have written about or otherwise demonstrated strategies they used in efforts to find a fulfilling career can be enriching. Chapter 2 highlights Luke Jackson's discovery of a love for visual arts like photography and computer graphics only after going through the struggle of trying on diverse career hats. Such exemplars can prompt discussions about struggles common to autistic people in finding a career path that is meaningful to them.

Interviewing professionals in the field of interest is another way that autistic youth can explore diverse career options. Such interviews can be prerecorded, written, dictated, or emailed; email holds the potential for sustained conversation between the interviewer (autistic student) and interviewee. In-person interviews can be conducive to the development of face-to-face communication and can be supported by peer or adult mentors, if necessary. Yet another avenue for exploring career ideas is field experience. Individuals, pairs, or small groups of students who share common interests can gain a sense of a particular field by shadowing professionals in the field and/or volunteering to do work in a place of interest. Such field experience can be integrated into a particular required course or fulfill a graduation requirement.

ENABLING MEANS OF EXPRESSION

The previous chapters reveal a number of ways that autistic people express themselves, emotionally and for the development and sharing of personal voice. Offering technological and hands-on experiences in schools can help students build a repertoire of strategies for expressing themselves creatively through a variety of media. Experiences with the tools and activities described below can be built into classroom and school curricula and can be available to all students, with the aim of expanding the ways in which they approach learning.

Letter Boards

Kedar, Mukhopadhyay, and Bonker attest to the empowerment that followed their learning to use letter boards to communicate their thoughts and ideas. Kedar, in particular, argues for a much broader use of letter boards for youth who do not speak. His witnessing of friends whom he observes to be "trapped" inside their minds has led to his very strong conviction that with use of letter boards, they too could develop their expressive potential. Schools can take heed, training some staff to specialize in the use of letter boards, with particular attention to how they can introduce the letter boards to nonverbal autistic students who have not yet begun to use them, as well as support the participatory and curricular inclusion of those who already do use them. Teachers likewise can lift the potential stigma of letter boards by explaining their use and function to the classroom community as a whole. In doing so, natural curiosity can be acknowledged and opportunities for collaboration could be opened up, as a nonverbal autistic student potentially could be matched with a number of possible partners in curricular work. This development would have the added benefits of facilitating social connection between neurodiverse peers and enabling the autistic student to reduce dependency on his or her one-on-one paraprofessional, which is important to the student's development of a strong identity (Kluth, 2003). Further, there could be an option to offer language credit (in the way that some schools offer credit to students who learn ASL) to students who might be interested in learning how to teach and use letter boards with students in younger grades. The younger autistic student would benefit from having a slightly older peer to work with, while the tutor would benefit from learning teaching skills and about qualities of autism and alternative means of expression.

Writing Devices

While a typing or computer lab can support the development of communication via writing, so too can low-tech devices. Simple Boogie Boards, which are LCD writing tablets used with a stylus, or whiteboards with markers can give primary students an opportunity to use gross motor skills to practice the writing of letters, numbers, and symbols. For older students, laptops and iPads or similar, less expensive devices (such as Chromebook or Samsung Galaxy Tab) can help in developing word processing skills. Technological features such as speech software (e.g., NaturalReader) could complement nonverbal students' typed work to present their ideas once they have been composed.

Writing Activities

It is clear that for many autistic people, writing is an expressive form that provides freedom to share their thoughts and ideas with others. Across the curriculum, teachers can offer opportunities to develop voice and perspective through poetry, current events, expository writing, song lyrics, blog writing, fiction writing, comics writing, and autobiography or memoir writing. Further, sharing of these written forms can support the discovery of shared interests between students and develop dynamic dialogue and conversation skills among class members.

One of the most successful activities I remember from my classroom teaching experience was the weekly current events reporting and sharing. At home, students researched a current event of interest, completed a report and summary of the event, and then brought their work to school, often with visual components such as photographs. We took a period each week to share current events, where similar topics segued into one another, and we always ended up having fruitful, meaningful discussions about a variety of local and worldwide happenings. The students (and I) looked forward to our current events activity every week, an essential and rich mainstay of our curricular diet. After the events had been shared and discussed, the reports were displayed on a bulletin board in the classroom, which reinforced students' learning and helped them build pride in their work.

The current events activity can be tailored to any age group, and the topics are compelling, for obvious reasons. Unlike historical events, current events bear relevance because of their immediacy and reflectiveness of a world in which students are enmeshed. Another attribute of current events is the element of choice. Students can choose to focus on absolutely any event of interest and can discern through their research how a favorite interest or topic relates to contemporary culture and society.

Students who find the physical act of writing difficult can rely on supports such as dictation (personal or software), extended time to complete work (one of the reasons I assigned current events on a weekly basis was to give students ample time to complete the task), typing labs, letter boards, and specific spaces in which to complete the work (e.g., home, a particular spot in the classroom or hallway). The freedom to work in spurts with breaks for movement also will help a number of students remain engaged in their work.

Visual Elements

Several of the people who are represented in this book make regular use of visual cues and aids in the process of creative engagement and learning in general (see Chapter 3). Mukhopadhyay's poems often center on specific objects in his visual atmosphere, such as the teacup in his kitchen and the markets of India. Bissonnette uses photography to document and remember the people who have made an impact on his life in significant ways. Gaines and Goldsmith use YouTube to archive pieces of creative performance. Classrooms and schools can include visual representations of creativity as part of the environmental landscape. Teachers can demonstrate and suggest the use of collage, posters, paintings, photographs, illustrations, computer graphics, YouTube, and other audiovisual media to support and enrich students' visual development and expression.

Inviting students to integrate visual elements into their curricular work gives them a chance to share their perspective in a nonlinguistic way. However, doing so can also aid their development of linguistic skills. Bissonnette's painting catalyzes his ability to describe his work in writing. YouTube gives Gaines the ability to showcase a number of communicative devices at once, including the uses of sign language and musical lyrics.

Music and Instruments

Goldsmith, Gaines, and Kedar demonstrate the importance of expressing themselves with music. For Goldsmith, music is an all-encompassing genre that has had far-reaching effects. For Gaines, music accompanies a love of theater performance and catalyzes her development of a number of ways to communicate with others. For Kedar, playing piano helps calm his emotions, channel his anxiety, and embed routine into his life in a way that feels constructive, revitalizing, and necessary for a sense of equilibrium. So, too, can music be integrated into classrooms to the benefit of all students' creative development. To enhance students' ability to play with diverse musical expressive forms, teachers can:

- Provide a listening station with headphones and easy volume control
- Allow for specific times when students can listen to their music with personal headphones
- Play music that appeals to all students
- Offer access to musical instruments (usually via a music class or, in older grades, the opportunity to play an instrument with the school band or orchestra)

While noise is a common sensitivity for autistic youth, noise buffers can be offered to those who need them, and teachers can ask the class to brainstorm about what types of music might support their ability to focus. The class can try to agree on a few types of music that appeal to all members.

Some other ideas of how a teacher might infuse music into curricular learning include:

- Asking students to connect subject learning with a musical component. For example, for a U.S. history study, students could choose to focus on the birth of jazz in particular metropolitan areas of the country (e.g., New Orleans or Harlem). Students could bring in pieces of jazz (either the lyrics or the recording, or both) that they like, to share with the class.
- Asking students to consider writing lyrics (perhaps, for example, with the caveat that the lyrics can be played by a class member who knows an instrument, thus forging a partnership between composer and performer)
- Inviting students to share their favorite songs with classmates, either by singing them or by playing them for the class
- Using dance and choreography to enhance curricular projects. For example, going back to the aforementioned U.S. history unit, students could choose to focus on a form of dance that either characterized or was popularized during a certain era of U.S. history, and then create, choreograph, and perform a dance to showcase that particular style. This particular choice lends itself to collaboration: A group of students interested in dance and performance could work together, each taking on different roles in the process of creating, choreographing, and performing (and videotaping if the performance is not going to be live) the dance.
- Giving students the opportunity to share the ways in which music is a tool for enriching their lives. For example, students can share

how music serves to energize them, alleviate stress, calm nerves, and/or promote focus.

Students with knowledge of particular musical instruments, or who sing, act, or dance, can share their skills with the class. For instance, a student who has tried out for a school musical could share with the class what he or she had to do to prepare for the audition and role. Embedding these types of activities regularly into curricular learning allows students to draw on their experiences with music (regardless of how formal or informal they might be) and underscores the ubiquitous nature of music in everyone's life.

There are, thus, a number of practices and tools that educators can adopt and provide to support autistic students' creative development alongside their neurotypical peers. Exploring the ideas set forth in this chapter can help teachers prepare for learning communities that recognize, appreciate, demonstrate, and support creativity in a variety of forms and encourage dynamic learning across curricular subjects. As teachers provide rich opportunities for all students to learn from and with one another about the ways that differences matter and about how differences can simultaneously connect and showcase unique individualities, they model a commitment to equity, democracy, and high expectations for all their students.

CHAPTER 5

Preparing for Creativity in Modernity and Beyond

Imagine what the world could be if everyone made even the slightest gain in their creative potentials. The total impact would be enormous and amazing.

—Mark A. Runco (2010)

In contemporary culture, imagination and creativity take various forms, ranging from the everyday to the artistic. Cultivating creative-thinking ability and expression can span the curricular subjects as well as extend beyond school walls to communities, both virtual and tangible. Supporting the development of all students' creative potentials requires educators to attend to different forms of creativity. In view of how engagement in arts-based creativity enriches the quality of life for many of the people featured in this book, schools make a wise investment when they choose to integrate into curricula arts-based opportunities for autistic youth. In this culminating chapter, I look to a present and ongoing cultural shift that requires greater development of citizens' creative- and critical-thinking abilities, and at the role that schools and classrooms have in supporting diverse students to prepare for contemporary and future cultural demands.

Within the realm of classroom learning, many of the features discussed in Chapter 4 will encourage students of all abilities to experiment with the arts (music, painting, photography, and so forth) and with diverse media. So, too, can extracurricular activities strengthen students' art-based creative abilities, as Goldsmith aptly describes in Chapter 3. Tito Mukhopadhyay, in an email exchange, similarly shared how his creative explorations with words and poetry happened outside of school contexts, in his "private domains" (personal communication, December 2, 2014). In the modern era, these types of creative integration maintain significance, mainly because they enrich the quality of life by offering a variety of forms and access points for human expression. In an era that is defined by technological advancement, the range of senses that are initiated in arts-based work provides authentic (versus virtual) connection with the world in which we live. Engagement with the arts also maintains significance because it catalyzes a range of skills and abilities that are transferable to other life contexts. The arts continue to provide fulfillment to people as both participants and observers.

The significance of educating for creativity in the modern age goes beyond a focus on the arts, though. Sawyer's (2010) discussion of the "creative age," which describes contemporary culture, commands a different view of the work educators have before them. With regard to preparing students for work in the world, contemporary educators play an integral role in helping develop the type of creativity that is, according to Boden (2004), "grounded in everyday abilities such as conceptual thinking, perception, memory, and reflective self-criticism" (p. 1). Developing creative-thinking habits and abilities is essential for navigating life's complexities. Of particular relevance, Seltzer and Bentley (1999) note that as jobs are becoming more knowledge-based and flexible, people are increasingly self-employed, working remotely, and doing more contract work. With this trend, they add, comes the need to know how to use skills across contexts and manage oneself and one's work.

The needs of contemporary culture also call for technological fluency. The past 20 years have been synonymous with tremendous technological evolution, and with that evolution new avenues for creative expression have emerged. People are now exercising creativity regularly through venues such as graphic design, software writing, online communication, social networking, and a multitude of other technology-based forms. Technological creativity aids science, medicine, and all kinds of research, where searching for, fusing, organizing, and accessing information are of direct relevance. Further, historically formal and hands-on arts such as painting and photography now rely on technology with regularity. (See, for instance, the multitude of software programs available to support photographic work. And on a more basic level, painters, illustrators, and artists often rely on the use of websites to showcase and promote their work.) Even everyday communication is increasingly reliant upon and enriched by technology. Email, which sometimes seems archaic, as well as blogs, online forums, listservs, tweeting, and texting are a few of the means by which we can connect and share ideas with one another. Technology plays a significant role in a new face of creativity.

At the same time, the regularity with which autistic students are joining their neurotypical peers in general education classrooms calls for a focus on rich educational experiences that prepare these youth to lead fulfilling lives and to contribute their abilities and skills in various societal roles. It is increasingly relevant that school-aged autistic individuals be prepared for a society that anticipates their contributions as adults. In October 2014, several members of Congress appealed to the Department of Health and Human Services (HHS) and the National Institutes of Health (NIH) to include more autistic people in the process of making decisions about autism-focused programs and autism research funded under the Autism CARES Act (passed earlier in the year). Funding allocated to areas of research that autistic people identify as significant to their lives remains low. For example, only 1.5% of funds are given to addressing the needs of autistic adults (Schakowsky, Castor, Duckworth, Speier, & Tonko, 2014). However, if the HHS and NIH heed the congressional appeal, action toward authentic inclusion of more autistic people in federal decisionmaking could be under way.

In efforts to prepare autistic youth for a society that increasingly will expect their participation and contributions, schools can help them develop their abilities and strengthen a range of dynamic skills in a number of ways, as discussed in the previous chapters. In authentic relationships with others, autistic youth can develop skills necessary to navigate and succeed in a world that demands the application of creative- and critical-thinking skills to address a range of vexing problems (e.g., social, technological, educational, economic, scientific). Both the changing needs of broad culture and the changing landscape of classrooms and schools provide unique opportunities for supporting the development of autistic students' creative potentials alongside and in conjunction with their neurotypical peers.

EDUCATING FOR A CREATIVE CULTURE

Adopting new approaches to educating students by focusing on cross-fertilization and thematic, multicontextual work sets the stage for educational experiences that are substantial, meaningful, and relevant. These approaches likewise offer greater flexibility and opportunity for depth of understanding than do traditional structures, where each subject is studied in isolation. Developing the capacity to fuse topics that traditionally are taught separately has the benefit of supporting the development of imagination. Allowing students to play with ideas and entertain possibilities, no matter how seemingly tangential, can spur interesting and novel ideas. These approaches also allow students' strengths to play a significant role, thus imbuing learning with inherent relevance. Work that bears relevance to one's life is internally rewarding (see Csikszentmihalyi, 1996). Because of their inherent motivational potential, these curricular approaches can be understood as measures that prevent idleness, boredom, and stagnation.

When educators attend to participatory preferences, maintain high expectations, and offer multiple tools to enhance learning, they open up possibilities for autistic students to thrive in school. That is, the combination of interest-rich, multicontext learning, flexible participatory structures, and multiple modalities with which to explore learning offers the promise of both igniting and sustaining autistic students' interest. Learning experiences that provide relevance and context work to draw students in, while modes of participation that support their abilities and reflect their preferences (e.g., the need to move around) serve to help sustain that initial engagement. The availability of tools and media such as music, computers, instruments, and other tactile, auditory, and visual elements contributes to sensorial, dynamic learning experiences. However, an imperative remains for educators to continually adjust their approaches as they observe changes and gather new information and knowledge about their students. Teaching with high expectations for all students requires fluidity, nonfixedness, ongoing reflection, and responsiveness (see Kluth, 2003).

DIVERSITY AS CREATIVITY

Students that make up the landscape of classrooms and schools likewise offer possibilities to enhance creative learning. Representing diverse ways of being, behaving, thinking, expressing, and perceiving, contemporary inclusive classrooms are rich with opportunities to teach and model how difference can breed creativity. Learning to understand phenomena from diverse perspectives, and learning from others' strengths and about others' struggles, expands students' well of knowledge and depth of understanding. It also has the benefit of preparing them to enter a world where inclusion is expected and routine, where people of diverse abilities work, vote, play, recreate, and live among one another in a more seamless, integrated way than in the past. Learning alongside peers of diverse abilities, students can teach one another coping strategies, learn about the body's connection to the mind, and appreciate that different people have different tolerances and sensitivities to certain sounds, textures, sights, smells, and so on. Teachers can help students (often autistic) who have a strong propensity to focus on particular topics of interest to channel those interests into individual or collaborative projects. In doing so, the value of maintaining focus and knowing a topic in depth is modeled. Likewise, with teacher support, students with fewer tendencies to focus intently on subjects can teach their interest-driven peers about flexibility, collaboration, and expanding areas of interest. Students who thrive on familiarity and are methodical in nature can be encouraged to approach their creative work with routine. In this way they may find, as many successful artists and thinkers do, a greater ability to focus and use time constructively. Teachers' transparency about the ways that certain habits enhance or hinder the ability to learn can help students see that, depending on the context, habits that are often understood as negative or nonproductive in fact can be beneficial and productive.

In an era where creative and critical thinking are foundational skills for success in multiple jobs, educators can use the composition of diverse classrooms to demonstrate how human variation itself represents creativity. They can enable students to discover how different ways of being and perceiving the world can breed new creative insights. They can highlight how bringing seemingly disparate people, ideas, experiences, and topics together can breed novelty. In short, teachers can help students realize how creativity comes alive in the "production of unusual associations" (Amabile, 1993, p. 179).

Moving beyond one's domain to explore ideas in diverse domains, or combining domains in efforts to understand phenomena in a new way or in new contexts, represents a way of bridging the old with the new and literally thinking outside of one's box of familiarity. Combining domains enriches pools of knowledge and fosters connections, and, in doing so, both broadens and constricts the world. Linking seemingly disparate ideas, people, and fields can multiply possibilities for novel ideas, solutions to problems, and insight. In terms of constricting, the fusion of diverse worlds can bring people together who otherwise may not have been brought together, thus increasing linkages between people in diverse fields. This process of increasing links between people in diverse fields decreases degrees of separation between people and promotes a sense that the world is smaller.

The role of technology in facilitating connections between disparate people and fields is of course critical. The Internet and social media have decreased degrees of separation between people (consider, for instance, the ways that LinkedIn, Facebook, YouTube, Twitter, Instagram, and other social media connect people with an ever-widening range of others). As this trend continues at a rapid rate, there are ever-increasing opportunities for people in far-reaching geographical locations and distinct fields to work in concert.

DISABILITY AS CREATIVITY

Similar to the ways in which features such as race, gender, and socioeconomics position one to experience life from different vantage points, so too does disability. While a diverse representation of these features adds to a community's enrichment, so too can it highlight the creative means by which people navigate the world in light of the difficulties they come across. Like other historically marginalized groups, disabled communities often share perceptions that veer from those which might be expected by majority culture. Disability scholar and activist Linton (1998) writes,

It is often startling to nondisabled people that many disabled people do not pine for the nondisabled experience, nor do they conceptualize disability as a potent determinant of their experience. Although . . . disabled people would celebrate the day of attaining equal social status, these are social and political determinants, not intrapsychic ones. (pp. 100–101)

This conception of disability helps to position disability as a feature by which the study of creativity can be expanded in new and exciting directions. A move away from purely medical interpretations of disability, or from those that associate disability with pity or misfortune, supports a focus on the many ways that disability experiences can cultivate creative insights and contributions. Disability necessarily breeds creativity because living within the constraints and limits posed by an able-bodied norm requires thoughtful and resourceful thinking skills. Disability scholar Garland-Thomson (2013) explains,

Disability can present us with an opportunity to find creative solutions to challenges of daily living by using the implements at hand and the capabilities we have to get what we want and need in life. Because disabled people live in a world that's not built with their bodies or capabilities in mind, they become experts in figuring out ways of doing things and strategies for getting the job done.

Adversity and the need to work in a culture of imposed limitations and constraints (including those social and political determinants that Linton refers to) are pivotal to creative decisionmaking. While scholars such as Linton and Garland-Thomson can attest to the creativity that is forged in the process of navigating a world designed primarily for the able-bodied, creativity scholars such as Beghetto and Kaufman (2010) concur with the general idea that limitations are often significant to creative development. Amabile's (1997) research shows this to be especially evident in the workplace, where factors such as time and the ability to collaborate with others play a role in one's capacity to meet creative goals. Similarly, Csikszentmihalyi's (1996) discussion of the Italian Renaissance emphasizes how the flurry of creativity in Florence was brought on in great part by limitations in artists' and engineers' understanding of construction strategies and dynamics, as well as a practical need for the completion of the Florence Cathedral's dome.

However, limitations are not the only quality that can lead to creative thinking, and as I have discussed throughout the book, disabled experiences offer new takes on phenomena that historically have been represented by the able-bodied. Baggs's (2007) video refuting the idea that a lack of speech is synonymous with a lack of intellectual ability reveals that creative impulses often are spurred by one's unique constitution and way of experiencing the world. What appear to be limitations to neuro-typical outsiders (e.g., a lack of conventional speech) are not necessarily so for Baggs, who wishes not to be someone different than who she is, but for her way of being to be recognized as human (see Chapter 1). The novelty with which she communicates and the substance of her insights command a focus on the ways that autism, rather than limiting her, em-powers her. Her expression likewise serves as an example of the vast and expansive ways that human beings express creativity and imagination.

SCHOOLS AND TEACHERS AS CREATIVE CATALYSTS

As communities that represent the diversity of their geographical sur-roundings, public schools have the unique opportunity and demanding task of supporting the growth and development of all their students. As mentioned in Chapter 1, all students under IDEA are entitled to a free and appropriate public education. However, this reality can seem forgot-ten in a system that so often sorts youth based on labels and needs that are perceived to be best met in segregated learning spaces. Contempo-rary public schools can be places that support movement into a future in which people of diverse abilities share equitable prospects for leading fulfilling lives. Encouraging the creative growth of all students is within the scope of public education. A focus on finding ways to integrate the perspectives and needs of diverse student bodies, with attention to the rapidly growing population of autistic students, is a pressing imperative for contemporary schooling.

The need to find ways to meaningfully engage autistic youth, and specifically to encourage their creative growth, is highlighted in an email exchange with Tito Mukhopadhyay. He wrote that he never felt the yearning to be included in public schools, because, he explained, "I never denied the fact that my faculties of mind and body experienced the sen-sory world differently" (personal communication, December 2, 2014). The public school, with its focus on students' conformity to a standard that was impossible for him, offered little relevance to Mukhopadhyay. The special education program he attended in the United States left him humiliated and idle, and in response to the school's lack of belief in his abilities, he daydreamed and escaped into his imagination. Yet in his adult years, Mukhopadhyay had a positive experience with inclusion in a col-lege-level course with Professor Ralph Savarese, who helped him further develop his writing abilities. Before that experience, Mukhopadhyay's creative pursuits were relegated, as mentioned previously, to his "private domains" (personal communication, December 2, 2014). Mukhopadhy-ay's insights bring attention to the monumental role of context. If schools were poised to expect and anticipate diversity of experiences of body and mind, such as those often represented by autistic youth, it is far more likely that autistic youth in fact would want to be included in classrooms and schools with their neurotypical peers. Mukhopadhyay had to wait until adulthood to enjoy a school-based creative learning experience that was inclusive. However, with thoughtful curricular planning and school-wide policies that support the well-being of a diverse student body, it is possible for contemporary autistic youth to begin their educational lives with similarly rich experiences.

In light of the reality that many schools continue to teach in ways that align with ideals of a bygone (industrial) era, teachers and administrators have an important role in the development of educational approaches that prepare all youth for a culture that requires their critical- and creative-thinking abilities. The significance of teachers in helping youth of all abilities work toward their potentials and prepare for fulfilling lives cannot be overstated. Policy and administrative support of teachers' efforts underlie the building of strong inclusive schools. Anti-bullying campaigns, district professional development that addresses issues and needs common to autistic youth, as well as neurodiversity awareness initiatives and site-specific appropriate support staff are all examples of measures that position schools to authentically integrate autistic students. Collaboration in the forms of parent/caregiver involvement and the inclusion of voices of autistic constituents is critical and further strengthens these measures.

Meaningful learning, the kind that relates to one's life and enriches one's pool of knowledge of a topic or issue that is provocative to him or her, often is prompted by a sense of connection to one's community. In classrooms and schools, where most children and youth spend a large percentage of their lives, students interact in a multitude of exchanges with their teachers and peers each day. By virtue of this reality, these relationships are pivotal for forming trusting communities. While policy and administrative support underlie student success, teachers, at the helm, are in a particularly advantageous position to get to know each student as well as the classroom community as a whole. Acting on their in-depth knowledge of students to steer them toward fuller development of their potentials is no easy job, yet it is one that can be immensely rewarding.

To illuminate the unique role that teachers have in awakening creativity in their students, I close with an anecdote that Vygotsky (1967/2004) references about the novelist Tolstoy. At some point in his life, Tolstoy worked with peasant children, teaching them to write about their lives, which they had never done before. They wrote of things that excited them, about things that were close to their hearts and minds, about topics of great relevance to them. Vygotsky shares how Tolstoy believed that "education ruins rather than improves people; teaching and instructing the child is impossible and senseless" (p. 50). However, what Tolstoy illustrated in his story about teaching the children was quite the opposite. He noted how the children were brimming with excitement and enlivened by their newfound abilities and growth as creative writers. As a person in a "teacher" role (although he likely would not have described himself as such), Tolstoy likewise experienced feelings of joy and fulfillment in supporting the students in their autobiographical work. He said of their writing, "I never encountered anything like these pages in all of Russian literature" (p. 49). Tolstoy's story attests to the idea that in educational contexts, bringing new information and ideas into the world is a result of individuals, often a teacher and his or her students, working in concert. It also brings to mind Runco's (2010) sentiment at the opening of this chapter, which suggests the potential for powerful cumulative change if all people could develop their creative abilities.

While "teacher" can take many forms, including mentor, caregiver, parent, clergy, counselor, administrator, extended family, and a host of other community members, it is clear that the role is powerful. In schools, educators bear a responsibility and a tremendous opportunity to facilitate learning experiences that incite, excite, spur, drive, engage, and sustain the imaginations of the youth that fill their classrooms. When helping students recognize and develop their creative abilities, teachers support habits of body and mind that build fulfilling lives.

Appendix: Notes on Methodology

My aim in this book was to explore the relationship between autism, creativity, and education. I wanted to forefront the perspectives of autistic people and their allies and, guided by the insights evoked from these data sources, suggest ways for educators to support the creative development of the autistic youth who populate their classrooms and schools. The methods of data collection and analysis that I used thus were chosen for their potential to allow a qualitative exploration of the relationship between autism, creativity, and education from the perspective of autistic people and their allies, and for their potential to inform specific applications for classroom use. My methods of data collection and analysis are borrowed from ethnographic tradition (see Denzin & Lincoln, 2003; Marshall & Rossman, 1999). My data came from interviews, artifacts, as well as scholarly, creative, and autobiographical writing and documentary. Together, these sources offered ample insight and information about several key qualities (or themes) that are significant for supporting the creative development of autistic youth in schools.

THE DATA SOURCES

In Chapter 2, I chose to focus on scholarly, creative, and autobiographical writing of autistic people and their allies because these data sources were compelling in their ability to provide exemplars of the sort of everyday, resourceful creativity in which autistic people engage. In some of the cases, I had familiarity with the work, but through my research I also learned of a number of new voices, such as Ido Kedar, Elizabeth Bonker, Naoki Higashida, and R. Daniel Linneman. I wanted the book to center the perspectives of autistic voices, and I wanted the data sources I chose to highlight creative use of one's resources. Each of the pieces featured in Chapter 2 met these criteria, and resoundingly so. They provided a multitude of insights and ideas about the ways that autistic people use creativity to navigate everyday complexities of life.

My decision to invite the people who are featured in Chapter 3 to contribute to the book originated in my belief that, in the words of qualitative researcher Valenzuela (1999), relationships form "the basis for all learning" (p. 61). Henry Goldsmith, Sarah Gaines, and Vincent Mazzone are three people I have known for over a decade, and they have known one another for even longer. For them to have familiarity with one another and with me was an important element of the data collection, because I believed that there would be a degree of trust among the group that otherwise might not exist among four strangers. My witnessing their creative development over the years, as I shared earlier, inspired my choice to pursue this book in the first place. Their active and consistent pursuit of lives that enfold their creative interests struck (and continues to strike) me as avenues rich with possibilities for insight into the relationship between autism, creativity, and education.

The other artists in Chapter 3 are people I have "known" for years as well, although not in a personal way. I have read and familiarized myself with the writing and artistic works of Tito Mukhopadhyay and Larry Bissonnette through my scholarly work and have had the opportunity to see Bissonnette participate in a discussion about his role in the documentary *Wretches and Jabberers* in 2011. Mukhopadhyay and I shared several emails over the course of my working on this book, because in reading his work I had questions with regard to his thinking on several topics. My personal experience in dialogue with Mukhopadhyay is recent, having spanned the past 2 years.

PARTICIPANT CONSENT, EMAIL DIALOGUING, VERIFICATION

In early 2013, I reached out to Mazzone, Gaines, and Goldsmith to gauge their interest in participating in a group email dialogue around the topics of autism, creativity, and education. Without the liberty to meet in person (we four lived in different geographical locations), I thought that a group email discussion would be conducive to building on one another's ideas and hoped that the online forum would allow us the freedom and flexibility to contribute our ideas and responses when it worked for us. Flexibility was an important feature because all of the participants lead very busy lives and were, at the time, in college.

I received affirmative responses from all three and gained their written consent to participate in a dialogue and to contribute artifacts that eventually would find their way into this book. I initiated an email (re) introduction in March 2013. While the participants already knew one another, it had been years since each went his or her own way, to pursue different life paths. I wanted everyone to know where each person was in his or her life, what they were working on, and what their near futures

held for them. After the introductory emails, we began our email dialogue, and I started the discussion by asking the participants to respond to
a few questions, such as:

- What comes to mind when you think of the word *autism*?
- What comes to mind when you think of the word *creativity*?
- How do these words intersect for you?

After the initial prompts, our conversation was built on ideas that
each had expressed. For instance, Mazzone mentioned that autism had
its benefits and its drawbacks for him with regard to his creativity. So, as
a way to engage the others' perceptions with regard to that idea, I highlighted his insight and asked the group if they could relate and, if so, how.
Our conversations thus were not hedged by prescribed questions I had;
rather, they developed organically as relevant, significant, interesting topics surfaced among the four of us.

While participants typically remembered to hit "reply all" each time
they submitted a response, there were several times when they responded
only to me, which initiated further prompting from me to have everyone
"reply all" with each response submission. In addition, participants took
different amounts of time to contribute responses, so although we continued to have a group email dialogue, at times the dialogue existed between
myself and one or two of the participants, with the other(s) chiming in
when prompted by me. Also, as facilitator to the conversation, although
I explicitly couched the dialogue as a group conversation, I realized that
most of the time participants directed their responses to me and rarely
directed a response at another participant. While this development might
have suggested that the participants were not learning from and building
upon one another's ideas, I reconsidered that judgment in light of the reality that regardless of the way in which they contributed their ideas, each
continually contributed thoughts that were rich, personal, and novel.

Our email dialogue continued through the summer of 2013, with follow-ups (usually to individual participants) continuing for months after.
In the 4 months (March–June) that we shared the group email dialogue,
we discussed topics as they grew out of prior discussions, such as:

- Stepping outside of one's comfort zone to learn new skills
- Managing stress, frustration, and other emotions
- The roles of familiarity, routines, and interests in creativity

In the summer of 2013, I asked each participant to send me artifacts
of his or her creative work. For this, each sent work samples such as illustrations and YouTube videos to me individually, and individual conversations between me and each participant ensued. This marked the end of

our group dialogue and the beginning of more individualized discussions based on the work each submitted.

Interviewing participants in person in a structure similar to a focus group likely would have yielded conversations that were enriched by the added dimensions of nonverbal communication, responding to ideas in real time, and perhaps a deepened sense of trust that often builds when people spend time in a physical space together. However, given the geographical constraints, the limit on participants' time, the flexibility I wanted the participants to have with response time, and participants' savvy ability and comfort with technology, email dialoging proved a constructive structure for the data collection.

IDENTIFICATION OF THEMES, ORGANIZATION, AND ANALYSIS

In Chapter 2, I organized the discussion of the various writing I reviewed and analyzed, using themes that were common to the distinct genres of writing. For instance, in my review of scholarly work, there were clear instances of creative resistance and responsive expression was evidenced in several cases. These themes lend organizational structure to my discussion of the scholarly literature. Likewise, in autism autobiography, the writers converged on a number of ideas, and these ideas (e.g., need for systems of support; drive for self-expression) structure the analysis and discussion of that section.

In Chapter 3, I used the email dialogues, the artifacts, as well as poetry and painting from other sources (e.g., books, documentaries) to discern common themes among the data. These themes provide the organizational structure for my analysis and discussion of significant elements of the artistic processes of autistic people. With regard to Henry Goldsmith, Sarah Gaines, Vincent Mazzone, and Tito Mukhopadhyay (whom I also gained written consent from), I frequently checked in to verify my interpretations of ideas they had expressed and at times to ask them to divulge in greater depth about an idea that seemed especially interesting. For Larry Bissonnette, the film documentary *Wretches and Jabberers* provided a dynamic and rich resource that complemented his paintings, which I discussed in this chapter.

References

Amabile, T. M. (1993). What does a theory of creativity require? *Psychological Inquiry, 4*(2), 179–237.

Amabile, T. M. (1997). Motivating creativity in organizations: On doing what you love and loving what you do. *California Management Review, 40*(1), 39–58.

Amabile, T .M., Hadley, C. N., & Kramer, S. J. (2002). Creativity under the gun. *Harvard Business Review, 80*(8), 52–61.

American Psychiatric Association. (1980). *Diagnostic and statistical manual of mental disorders* (3rd ed.). Washington, DC: Author.

American Psychiatric Association. (2000). *Diagnostic and statistical manual of mental disorders* (Rev. 4th ed.). Washington, DC: Author.

American Psychiatric Association. (2013). *Diagnostic and statistical manual of mental disorders* (5th ed.). Washington, DC: Author.

Asperger, H. (1991). "Autistic psychopathology" in childhood. In U. Frith (Ed. & Trans.), *Autism and Asperger syndrome* (pp. 32–97). Cambridge, UK: Cambridge University Press. (Original work published 1944)

Autism Self-Advocacy Network. (2015a). *About autism.* Available at autisticadvocacy.org/about-autism/

Autism Self-Advocacy Network. (2015b). *Position statements.* Available at autisticadvocacy.org/policy-advocacy/position-statements/

Baer, J., & Garrett, T. (2010). Teaching for creativity in an era of content standards and accountability. In R. A. Beghetto & J. C. Kaufman (Eds.), *Nurturing creativity in the classroom* (pp. 6–23). Cambridge, UK: Cambridge University Press.

Baggs, A. (2007, January 14). *In my language* [Video file]. Available at www.youtube.com/watch?v=JnylM1hI2jc

Baldwin, A. Y. (2010). Creativity: A look outside the box in classrooms. In R. A. Beghetto & J. C. Kaufman (Eds.), *Nurturing creativity in the classroom* (pp. 73–87). Cambridge, UK: Cambridge University Press.

Baron-Cohen, S., Leslie, A. M., & Frith, U. (1985). Does the autistic child have a "theory of mind"? *Cognition, 21*, 37–46.

Beghetto, R. A., & Kaufman, J. C. (2010). Broadening conceptions of creativity in the classroom. In R. A. Beghetto & J. C. Kaufman (Eds.), *Nurturing creativity in the classroom* (pp. 191–205). Cambridge, UK:

Cambridge University Press.

Beghetto, R. A., & Kaufman, J. C. (2013). Fundamentals of creativity. *Educational Leadership, 70*(5), 10–15.

Bianco, M., Carothers, D. E., & Smiley, L. R. (2009). Gifted students with Asperger syndrome. *Intervention in School and Clinic, 44*(4), 206–215.

Biklen, D. (2005). *Autism and the myth of the person alone.* New York, NY: New York University Press.

Biklen, D., & Burke, J. (2006). Presuming competence. *Equity and Excellence in Education, 39*(2), 166–175.

Bissonnette, L. (2005). Letters ordered through typing produce the story of an artist stranded on the island of autism. In D. Biklen, *Autism and the myth of the person alone* (pp. 172–182). New York, NY: New York University Press.

Bissonnette, L. (2013, October 30). Words from the road: Edgewood College and California State at Northridge October 2013 [Blog post]. Available at wretchesandjabberers.org/larry/index.php

Blackman, L. (2005). Reflections on language. In D. Biklen, *Autism and the myth of the person alone* (pp. 146–167). New York, NY: New York University Press.

Bock, M. (2001). SODA strategy: Enhancing the social interaction skills of youngsters with Asperger syndrome. *Intervention in School and Clinic, 36*(5), 272–278.

Boden, M. A. (2004). *The creative mind: Myths and mechanisms.* London, UK: Routledge.

Bonker, E. M., & Breen, V. G. (2011). *I am in here.* Grand Rapids, MI: Revell.

Breen, V., & Bonker, E. (2012). *When you finally find your voice, what do you most want to say?* [Video file]. Available at www.tedmed.com/talks/show?id=7301

Broderick, A., & Ne'eman, A. (2008). Autism as metaphor. *International Journal of Inclusive Education, 12*(5), 459–476.

Cain, S. (2012). *Quiet: The power of introverts in a world that can't stop talking.* New York, NY: Broadway Books.

Carrington, S., & Graham, L. (2001). Perceptions of school by two teenage boys with Asperger syndrome and their mothers: A qualitative study. *Autism, 5*(1), 37–48.

Carrington, S., Templeton, E., & Papinczak, T. (2003). Adolescents with Asperger syndrome and perceptions of friendship. *Focus on Autism and Other Developmental Disabilities, 18*(4), 211–218.

Carter, R. (2004). *Language and creativity: The art of common talk.* London, UK: Routledge.

Craig, J., & Baron-Cohen, S. (1999). Creativity and imagination in autism and Asperger syndrome. *Journal of Autism and Developmental Disorders, 29*(4), 319–326.

Csikszentmihalyi, M. (1996). *Creativity: Flow and the psychology of discovery and invention*. New York, NY: Harper Perennial.

Csikszentmihalyi, M. (1997). Happiness and creativity: Going with the flow. *The Futurist, 31*(5), 8–12.

Denzin, N. K., & Lincoln, Y. S. (2003). *The landscape of qualitative research: Theories and issues* (2nd ed.). Thousand Oaks, CA: Sage.

Fairweather, E., & Cramond, B. (2010). Infusing creative and critical thinking into the curriculum together. In R. A. Beghetto & J. C. Kaufman (Eds.), *Nurturing creativity in the classroom* (pp. 113–141). Cambridge, UK: Cambridge University Press.

Fitzgerald, M. (2004). Autism and creativity: Is there a link between autism in men and exceptional ability? East Sussex, UK: Brunner-Routledge.

Fitzgerald, M. (2005). *The genesis of artistic creativity: Asperger's syndrome and the arts*. London, UK, & Philadelphia, PA: Jessica Kingsley.

Frith, U. (2003). *Autism: Explaining the enigma*. Oxford, UK: Blackwell.

Frith, U. (2004). Emanual Miller lecture: Confusions and controversies about Asperger syndrome. *Journal of Child Psychology and Psychiatry, 45*(4), 672–686.

Frugone, A. (2005). Salient moments in the life of Alberto, as a child, a youth, a young man. In D. Biklen, *Autism and the myth of the person alone* (pp. 185–197). New York, NY: New York University Press.

Furniss, G. (2009, May 1). Art lessons for a young artist with Asperger syndrome. *Art Education*, pp. 18–24.

Gaines, S. (2013, June 24). *"I believe" from the Book of Mormon in ASL* [Video file]. Available at www.youtube.com/watch?v=t4ThzWrqPkg

Garland-Thomson, R. (2013, January 17). Sex lessons. [Web log comment]. Available at www.huffingtonpost.com/rosemarie-garlandthomson/the-sessions-sex-surrogacy_b_2498357.html

Ghiselin, B. (1985). *The creative process: Reflections on invention in the arts and sciences*. Oakland, CA: University of California Press.

Goldsmith, H. (2010a, June 19). *SOR allstars with Joe Lynn Turner all right now* [Video file]. Available at www.youtube.com/watch?v=TgKgAAtSOIE

Goldsmith, H. (2010b, November 23). *We're not gonna take it—Dee Snider with the School of Rock all stars* [Video file]. Available at www.youtube.com/watch?v=WvY0akAaU0E

Grandin, T. (2006). *Thinking in pictures: And other reports from my life with autism*. New York, NY: Doubleday.

Grandin, T. (2013, November 19). *Temple Grandin: "The autistic brain"* [Video file]. Available at www.youtube.com/watch?v=MWePrOuSeSY

Gray, C. A. (1995). *Social stories unlimited: Social stories and comic strip conversations*. Jenison, MI: Jenison Public Schools.

Haddon, M. (2003). *The curious incident of the dog in the night-time*. New York, NY: Doubleday.

Happe, F., & Frith, U. (2010). *Autism and talent*. Oxford, UK: Oxford University Press.

Hay, I., & Winn, S. (2005). Students with Asperger's syndrome in an inclusive secondary school environment: Teachers', parents' and students' perspectives. *Australasian Journal of Special Education, 29*(2), 140–154.

Henderson, L. M. (2001). Asperger syndrome and gifted individuals. *Gifted Child Today, 24*(3), 28–35.

Higashida, N. (2013). *The reason I jump: The inner voice of a thirteen-year-old boy with autism*. New York, NY: Random House.

Humphrey, N., & Lewis, S. (2008). "Make me normal": The views and experiences of pupils on the autistic spectrum in mainstream schools. *Autism, 12*(1), 23–46.

Insel, T. R. (2007). Autism research at the National Institutes of Health. Available at www.hhs.gov/asl/testify/2007/04/t20070417a.html

Insel, T. R. (2012). Director's blog: Autism prevalence: More affected or more detected? Available at www.nimh.nih.gov/about/director/2012/autism-prevalence-more-affected-or-more-detected.shtml

Jackson, L. (2002). *Freaks, geeks, and Asperger syndrome*. London, UK, & Philadelphia, PA: Jessica Kingsley.

Jackson, L. (2006). *Crystalline lifetime: Fragments of Asperger syndrome*. London, UK, & Philadelphia, PA: Jessica Kingsley.

Jackson, L. (2012, December 12). *Jacqui and Luke Jackson talk about their experiences of autism in school and beyond* [Video file]. Available at www.youtube.com/watch?v=X9JOfPsu9kI

Jackson, M. (Director), & Ferguson, S. (Producer). (2010). *Temple Grandin* [Motion picture]. United States: HBO Films, Ruby Films.

Jorgensen, C. M. (2006). Facilitating student relationships: Fostering class membership and social connections. In C. M. Jorgensen & M. C. Schuh, *The inclusion facilitator's guide* (pp. 125–138). Baltimore, MD: Brookes.

Kagan, J., & Snidman, N. (2004). *The long shadow of temperament*. Cambridge, MA: Harvard University Press.

Kane, J. (2007). Poetry as right-hemispheric language. *PsyArt*. Available at www.psyartjournal.com/article/list/2007

Kanner, L. (1943). Autistic disturbances of affective contact. *Nervous Child, 2*, 217–250.

Kapp, S., & Ne'eman, A. (2012). *ASD in DSM-5: What the research shows and recommendations for change*. Available at autisticadvocacy.org/wp-content/uploads/2012/06/ASAN_DSM-5_2_final.pdf

Kaufman, J. C., & Beghetto, R. A. (2009). Beyond big and little: The four C model of creativity. *Review of General Psychology, 13*(1), 1–12.

Kaufman, W. E. (2012). DSM-5: *The new diagnostic criteria for autism spectrum disorders*. Available at www.autismconsortium.org/symposium-files/WalterKaufmannAC2012Symposium.pdf

Kedar, I. (2012). *Ido in autismland: Climbing out of autism's silent prison.* Publisher: Author.

Kluth, P. (2003). You're going to love this kid! Teaching students with autism in the inclusive classroom. Baltimore, MD: Brookes.

Leblanc, L., Richardson, W., & McIntosh, J. (2005). The use of applied behavioral analysis in teaching children with autism. *The International Journal of Special Education, 20*(1), 13–34.

Linneman, R. D. (2001). *Idiots: Stories about mindedness and mental retardation.* New York, NY: Peter Lang.

Linton, S. (1998). *Claiming disability: Knowledge and identity.* New York, NY: New York University Press.

Little, C. (2002). Which is it? Asperger syndrome or giftedness? Defining the differences. *Gifted Child Today, 25*(1), 28–63.

Lord, C. (2006). *Rules.* New York, NY: Scholastic.

Luckenbach, T. A. (1986). Encouraging "little-c" and "Big C" creativity. *Research Management, 29*(2), 9–10.

Marshall, C., & Rossman, G. B. (1999). *Designing qualitative research* (3rd ed.). Thousand Oaks, CA: Sage.

Mayer, M. (Director), & De Pincier, M., Urdang, L., & Vanech, D. (Producers). (2009). *Adam* [Motion picture]. United States: Olympus Pictures.

Merrotsy, P. (2013). A note on Big-C and little-c creativity. *Creativity Research Journal, 25*(4), 474–476.

Miller, A. L., Lambert, A. D., & Speirs Neumeister, K. L. (2012). Parenting style, perfectionism, and creativity in high-ability and high-achieving young adults. *Journal for the Education of the Gifted, 35*(4), 344–365.

Mitchell, D. (2013). Introduction. In N. Higashida, (Ed.), *The reason I jump: The inner voice of a thirteen-year-old boy with autism* (pp. vii–xvii). New York, NY: Random House.

Mukhopadhyay, T. R. (2008). *How can I talk if my lips don't move?* New York, NY: Arcade.

Mukhopadhyay, T. R. (2010). Five poems. *Disability Studies Quarterly, 30*(1). Available at dsq-sds.org/article/view/1192/1256

Mukhopadhyay, T. R. (2011). *The mind tree.* New York, NY: Arcade.

Mukhopadhyay, T. R., & Biklen, D. (2005). Questions and answers. In D. Biklen, *Autism and the myth of the person alone* (pp. 110–143). New York, NY: New York University Press.

Myles, B. S., & Simpson, R. L. (2001). Effective practices for students with Asperger syndrome. *Focus on Exceptional Children, 34*(3), 1–14.

Myles, B. S., & Simpson, R. L. (2002). Asperger syndrome: An overview of characteristics. *Focus on Autism and Other Developmental Disabilities, 17*(3), 132–137.

Nachmanovitch, S. (1990). *Free play: Improvisation in life and art.* New York, NY: Penguin Putnam.

Ogata, A. F. (2013). *Designing the creative child: Playthings and places in midcentury America.* Minneapolis, MN: University of Minnesota Press.

Osler, A., & Osler, C. (2002). Inclusion, exclusion, and children's rights: A case study of a student with Asperger syndrome. *Emotional and Behavioral Difficulties, 7*(1), 35–54.

Richards, R. (2010). Everyday creativity in the classroom: A trip through time with seven suggestions. In R. A. Beghetto & J. C. Kaufman (Eds.), *Nurturing creativity in the classroom* (pp. 206–234). Cambridge, UK: Cambridge University Press.

Riddle, C. A. (2013). The ontology of impairment: Rethinking how we define disability. In M. Wappett & K. Arndt (Eds.), *Emerging perspectives on disability studies* (pp. 23–40). New York, NY: Palgrave Macmillan.

Rosqvist, H. B. (2012). Practice, practice: Notions of adaptation and normality among adults with Asperger syndrome. *Disability Studies Quarterly, 32*(2). Available at dsq-sds.org/article/view/3191

Runco, M. A. (2010). Education based on a parsimonious theory of creativity. In R. A. Beghetto & J. C. Kaufman (Eds.), *Nurturing creativity in the classroom* (pp. 235–251). Cambridge, UK: Cambridge University Press.

Savarese, R. J. (2008, Spring). The lobes of autobiography: Poetry and autism. *Stone Canoe, 2,* 61–77.

Savarese, R. J. (2010). Toward a postcolonial neurology: Autism, Tito Mukhopadhyay, and a new geo-poetics of the body. *Journal of Literary and Cultural Disability Studies, 4*(3), 273–290.

Sawyer, R. K. (2010). Learning for creativity. In R. A. Beghetto & J. C. Kaufman (Eds.), *Nurturing creativity in the classroom* (pp. 172–190). Cambridge, UK: Cambridge University Press.

Schakowsky, J., Castor, K., Duckworth, T., Speier, J., & Tonko, P. (2014). Letter to Secretary Burwell and Director Collins. Available at autisticadvocacy.org/wp-content/uploads/2014/10/10.28.14-Autism-CARES-Implementation-Letter.pdf

Seltzer, K., & Bentley, T. (1999). *The creative age: Knowledge and skills for the new economy.* London, UK: Demos.

Sinclair, J. (1993). Don't mourn for us. *Our Voice, 1*(3). Available at www.autreat.com/dont_mourn.html

Stein, M. I. (1953). Creativity and culture. *Journal of Psychology, 36,* 311–322.

Sternberg, R. J. (2010). Teaching for creativity. In R. A. Beghetto & J. C. Kaufman (Eds.), *Nurturing creativity in the classroom* (pp. 394–414). Cambridge, UK: Cambridge University Press.

Synopsis of *Wretches and jabberers.* (2015). Available at wretchesandjabberers.org/synopsis.php

Valenzuela, A. (1999). *Subtractive schooling: U.S.-Mexican youth and the politics of caring.* Albany, NY: State University of New York Press.

Vygotsky, L. S. (2004). Imagination and creativity in childhood. (M. E. Sharpe, Inc., Trans.). *Journal of Russian and East European Psychology, 42,* 7–97. (Original work published 1967)

Wappett, M., & Arndt, K. (Eds.). (2013). *Emerging perspectives on disability studies.* New York, NY: Palgrave Macmillan.

Wing, L. (2005). Reflections on opening Pandora's box. *Journal of Autism and Developmental Disorders, 35*(2), 197–203.

Winter-Messiers, M. A. (2007). From tarantulas to toilet brushes: Understanding the special interest areas of children and youth with Asperger syndrome. *Remedial and Special Education, 28*(3), 140–153.

Wurzburg, G. (Director), & Biklen, D., & Wurzburg, G. (Producers). (2011). *Wretches and jabberers* [Documentary]. United States: State of the Art.

Xu, J. (2012, September 27). Autism as an identity, not a disease. *The Michigan Daily Review.* Available at www.michigandaily.com/arts/melanie-yergeau-autistic-self-advocacy

Index

About the Author

Carrie C. Snow, EdD, is an independent scholar interested in the intersection of autism, schooling, and creativity. Her past work includes classroom teaching as a special educator, university teaching, rapporteur for the Columbia University Seminar on Disability Studies, and several years in New York City public schools supporting the development of student teachers. She completed a master's degree in Learning Dis/Abilities and a doctoral degree in Curriculum and Teaching at Teachers College, Columbia University, where she was a recipient of several scholarships, including teaching and leadership opportunities. She currently serves on the editorial board for the journal *Disability Studies Quarterly* (DSQ) and has published work in *DSQ, The Encyclopedia of American Disability History,* and, recently, a chapter in *Emerging Perspectives on Disability Studies* (2013). She lives in Seattle with her husband and two young children.